How To Vacation & Travel Safely

How To Vacation & Travel Safely

... and Come Back Alive

Earnest Hart, Jr.

Copyright © 2011 by Earnest Hart, Jr.

Library of Congress Control Number: 2011918260
ISBN: Hardcover 978-1-4653-7889-7
Softcover 978-1-4653-7888-0
Ebook 978-1-4653-7890-3

All rights reserved. No part of this book may be reproduced or transmitted in any form or by any means, electronic or mechanical, including photocopying, recording, or by any information storage and retrieval system, without permission in writing from the copyright owner.

This book was printed in the United States of America.

To order additional copies of this book, contact:
Xlibris Corporation
1-888-795-4274
www.Xlibris.com
Orders@Xlibris.com
103342

Contents

Preface: Prisoner from the Land of the Free................................9
Chapter 1:   The Realities of Traveling in The New Millennium.... 15
Chapter 2:   Home Safety While You Are Away 20
Chapter 3:   Pretravel Safety... 26
Chapter 4:   Car Safety on the Road 32
Chapter 5:   Bus and Train Safety 39
Chapter 6:   Airport Safety... 42
Chapter 7:   Safely Getting to Your Destination 49
Chapter 8:   Hotel and Motel Safety.. 54
Chapter 9:   Cruise Ship Safety... 61
Chapter 10: Know the Rules before You Go 66
Chapter 11: Safely Traveling Overseas... 74
Chapter 12: Business Travel Safety.. 86
Chapter 13: Staying "Street Smart" in Unfamiliar Cities............. 121
Chapter 14: Gender—and Age-Specific Travel Safety 138
Chapter 15: Personal Safety and Self-defense............................. 156
Conclusion 181
Synopsis 183

About the Author

Earnest Hart Jr. is a world-class martial arts champion, corporate protection and self-protection expert, physical fitness trainer, actor, and seminar specialist. In the ring, he earned a reputation as the man to beat and was considered one of the most formidable competitors of his day.

As a teenager, he trained in several fighting arts which included karate, boxing, judo, jujitsu, and wrestling and had to constantly test his skills on the streets, living and hanging out in some of the toughest neighborhoods and housing projects in St. Louis, MO. At eighteen, these skills were put to task as he shot onto the kickboxing scene. At age twenty-one, Hart won his first World PKA Kickboxing title (among his many other accomplishments). Hart is the first American ever to win four kickboxing titles.

A multitalented martial artist, Hart holds black belts in fifteen different styles. They include Yoshukai karate, 8th degree, under Rich Hootselle; jujitsu, 7th degree, under Mel Brown; judo, 6th degree, under Avis Dunbar; Tae Kwon Do, 6th degree, under Frank Babcock; and kajukenbo, 4th degree, under John Short. Over the years, Hart has trained and perfected several fighting arts such as savate, shootfighting, and shootboxing, and trained in various forms of weaponry such as edged weapons, stick fighting, and firearms. He is also the highest ranking teacher at 10th degree in the American Fighting Arts School of Martial Arts and has been named one of the "Top Ten Kickboxers of All Time" by *Inside Karate* magazine.

His brilliant career includes motivational speaking and seminars. The topics range from "Just Say No to Drugs" to rape awareness clinics. He has given seminars for people such as Chuck Norris and Pat Johnson, in addition to training some of the country's top athletes like Baseball Hall of Famer Ozzie Smith of the St. Louis Cardinals, and O. J. Anderson of the New York Giants. Hart was the official martial arts trainer for the 1999-2000 Super Bowl Champion St. Louis Rams. In addition to keeping these gridiron superstars in prime physical condition, he taught them how to apply various martial art techniques to the game of football. The Rams's coaches and players agree that this unique program is an important part of the Rams's fitness program and game plan.

Hart's talents have been used for acting, stunt work, and outstanding fight scenes in a variety of movies including *To Live and Die in LA*, *Karate Kid III*, *Mortal Kombat*, and as one of Mr. Freeze's ice thugs in *Batman and Robin*. He has worked with Arnold Schwarzenegger, George Clooney, Pat Morita, and Willem Dafoe.

His career has taken him to faraway lands such as Japan, where he became the only Westerner to train the emperor's personal security forces, to Monte Carlo, where he demonstrated his art in a Royal Command Performance for Prince Rainer and Princess Grace. He was also the first person ever to fight and defend his title in Nashville, Tennessee, at the legendary Grand Ole Opry.

Over the years, Hart has provided executive protection to his elite clients, in addition to teaching and training executive protection specialists on the finer points of personal protection and CQC (Close Quarter Combat). Hart also provides personal safety and training services to a variety of clients and teaches self-protection courses to individuals, schools, and corporations.

Preface

Prisoner from the Land of the Free

I thought nightmares only happen while sleeping, but I had to live through one during August 1977. My kickboxing career was taking off, and I was slated to fight on national TV in October of the same year (only the third person, and the first African—American to do so in the history of the sport). Having trained and fought in the streets for the past twelve years and having to deal with being shot at, stabbed, and cut several times with knives and bottles, I felt complete confidence in who I was and my ability to handle anything that came my way. When one is known for being one of the toughest men in the world, why not be confident?

One Night in Bangkok

An old friend was in a bind and invited me to be a guest at a kickboxing event in Bangkok, Thailand. The big event needed a rising star in the sport, and naturally, I fit the bill. When they sent a one-way plane ticket, most people would have seen the red flags, but I shrugged it off. What could possibly go wrong? Kickboxing champion + handsome young man = invincible . . . right?

When I landed in Bangkok, I soon understood why someone wrote the lyrics, "One night in Bangkok and the tough guys tumble." My "friend" failed to realize that I was already under contract to fight on American TV and so neglected to tell the Thai promoters who had arranged my fight with a champion Thai boxer. As they drove me to my hotel, there were huge billboards with my picture on them advertising the bout. My mug was everywhere.

After entering the Thai stadium, it was immediately clear to me that I was in over my head. Instead of simply being a guest, the promoters told me that I would have to fight in two days. When I jumped from my chair and objected, two military guards approached me with machine guns. This was only the beginning of the nightmare, and it got worse.

Back at the hotel, I decided to try and get to the U.S. embassy in any way possible. However, my passport and visa had been confiscated. I tried to call the embassy, but I couldn't get a call out; my phones had been rigged to prevent me from calling out of the country. When I tried to sneak out, there were guards at my door. I was told that I couldn't leave the hotel. There were three other American fighters that had been there much longer than I had and were not allowed to leave the country until they fought several times to work off the expense of bringing them there. This was the first time in my adult life that that I felt I was not in control of a situation.

The day of the fights came quickly. My plan was to go in, take care of their Thai champion, and then return home.

Negative. When we got to the stadium, we were told by the Thai gentleman assigned to us that if we won our matches, we would not be leaving Thailand for a while. He also said, "Thai prisons make U.S. prisons seem like Girl Scout camps." We were stunned.

To give you a little background on Thai boxing, they begin training at a very young age. Fights take place every day of the year. Thai boxing to Thailand is what soccer is to Europe; the

Thai people live and breathe the sport. Participants are known to be some of the toughest fighters in the world. Thai boxers use knees and elbows from close range, as well as devastating muay thai kicks at long range, which can drop an opponent instantly.

Without much time to think about it, the first American went into the ring. The "tough" Thai fighter was dealing powerful kicks to the legs. Because the American was not fighting as hard as he could, he took a lot of punishment, and by the fourth round he simply took a standing eight count and was counted out. As he walked back to our room, he was pelted with flying objects and people began attacking him from the audience. As I was about to fight, I was told, "You had better put up a better fight than the last guy."

In the first round, I dropped my opponent three times, but he got up each time. In the second round, I dropped him again and then I began to get scared. I couldn't afford to hit him too hard and knock him out. Just like the other fighter from the USA, I started to take too much punishment from the kicks to my legs, and by the fourth round I had my corner man throw in the towel. My legs were killing me. I had to carry my opponent through the bout, but the leg kicks were too much to handle, and I didn't need permanent injuries.

Shortly thereafter, I headed out the side door with the other fighters and the Thai assistants who had been assigned to us. As we stepped out, there were several hundred Thai fight fans waiting for us. We thought they were *our* fans, but without warning they began to attack. Running to the van, I had to force my way through a gauntlet of punches and kicks. Once we got inside, they tried to rock the van as we were taking off. My heart was beating a hundred miles an hour.

Back at the hotel, the promoter came to meet us and said he had bad news. "We did not make enough money to pay you." This was a ploy they used to get the price down on the fighters. They said they would try to have our cash in a day or so.

After three days we still hadn't heard from the promoters, but I noticed there were no longer any guards watching us. Bored and needing a change of pace, I found a cab and began to explore the city of Bangkok. I visited temples, museums, and other places of interest. As the late afternoon rolled around, things began to change. People knew who I was and would wave and talk to me. Most people were very nice and accommodating, while a few were not. Throughout the day, complete strangers would challenge me on the street. Finally, a gang of men attacked me.

As I was fighting, one of the attackers came at me with a type of sword I had never seen. Luckily for me, my cab pulled up, and I was able to jump in and get away.

Later, I asked my cabdriver to take me back to my hotel. He started to scream at me and claimed we had to get off the streets. Due to the country's curfew, he didn't have time to get me back to my hotel. Everyone except the military had to clear the streets because of the political problems Thailand was having at the time. The cabbie dropped me off at an opium den/prostitution house, explaining before he drove away that he would pick me up at a certain time in the early morning. I went from spending nights at a great hotel to begrudgingly sleeping at "The Opium/Prostitution Inn." Beam me up, anybody!

I didn't get a bit of sleep that night. I sat up in my bed with my back to the wall, looking at the door, and hoping no one would come through it. I started to wonder if I was ever going to get back to the U.S. alive. No one outside of Thailand really knew where I was. The most important questions I went over many times during that night were, "How could I have prevented this from happening, and how do I get out of this situation?"

The cabdriver picked me up the next morning as promised and drove me back to the hotel. Later that afternoon, the promoters showed up with a suitcase full of cash. I figured since I was going to get paid, maybe the whole experience wasn't so bad. As they stacked the money on the table, I started to rub my hands together.

Then came the next surprise: they started deducting for my expenses—airfare, room, transportation, food, etc. When it was all finished, I was upset but couldn't do anything about it. "Are you ready to go home?" they asked. I didn't even have to answer that question.

I was allowed to leave with one other fighter, and we were on our way to the airport within the next hour. Our passports were returned and our visas reissued. When I reached the airport and went through customs, I was taken to a back room and interrogated. After two hours of questioning, they "relieved" me of about five hundred dollars. They said it was taxes due for training equipment I purchased which actually cost forty (American) dollars . . . And you thought our taxes were high!

A million things ran through my mind on the last leg of the trip home from Thailand. I realize now that I was actually a hostage. I was at their mercy, and they could have just as easily thrown me in jail or killed me, and there wasn't a thing anyone could have done about it. When my plane landed in Los Angeles, there were several people waiting for us, anxious to find out what really happened. After we told them our story, they were concerned but not completely surprised.

Later, I discovered that the Thai promoters planned to use my loss as a way to showcase their fighters on American TV. Since I was about to be broadcast into American homes, they wanted to steal the wind beneath my wings and place it under theirs. Unfortunately, for them, their wings got clipped.

The next month I won my first of four World Kickboxing titles and continued to travel all over the world. This incident laid the groundwork for me to not only become a better fighter in the ring, but to be made aware that while America is a great place to live, there are dangers that we face here which need to be addressed, and even more so when we travel outside our country.

This book, *How to Vacation and Travel Safely . . . and Come Back Alive*, is a result of my years of experience of traveling across the globe and extensive research in the areas of safety and protection. When reading, begin by taking one topic of interest at a time and casually learn the chapter information. Learn how you can apply the skills to both you and your family. Keep it simple.

Due to the nature of my profession, I have learned things about protecting one's self that most people have probably never even considered. In this book, you will learn the realities of what threats exist to you and your family and how best to deal with them so that when you do decide to vacation and travel . . . you will definitely come back alive.

Chapter One

The Realities of Traveling in The New Millennium

Traveling is a way of life. It is the means by which we get to work, visit friends and family, and see the world. Whether traveling on foot, by train, on a plane, or in an automobile, it is something we do on a daily basis, often with little forethought. Problems are encountered because the world of travel is now a playground for criminals and terrorists. "Paradise," or wherever else you plan to travel to, could possibly be where they catch you off guard and rob you of your possessions, your decency, and even your life.

As a person on the go, you should face the realities of traveling and must commit to making your personal safety a top priority. In order to do so, you need to be realistic and open-minded to new ways of thinking. Admit that your safety is not guaranteed and be willing to educate yourself about the steps necessary to stay safe in today's environment. Take the time to create a simple game plan that you and your family can easily learn and follow in emergency situations.

Before you begin taking steps toward a new perspective on safety, you must first learn the significance of four important principles:

1. Sense of Awareness
2. Proper Mind-set
3. Mental Preparation
4. Confidence

Sense of awareness enables you to see and think about your safety and that of your family on a regular basis. It allows you to develop a "sixth sense" or the ability to feel and see problems before they happen, which is otherwise known as "street smarts."

Having the *proper mind-set* means being able to develop a mental understanding that you and you alone are responsible for your safety. Know that you must do whatever it takes to protect yourself no matter where you are. The police can't always be depended upon; nice criminals and con artists don't always commit crimes when the police are around. Furthermore, you can't depend on your friends or strangers if they are with you during a crisis. Your friends may be less prepared to deal with a situation than you are, and strangers usually don't want to get involved in a criminal situation, due to the fear of violence and legal ramifications. Mentally, you must be totally responsible for your safety, because this is the only way you can truly feel safe.

Mental preparation is the ability to visualize potentially dangerous situations, and ensure that a preconceived mental game plan is in place that offers a variety of safety options. Making mental preparations regarding safety before leaving on a vacation or family outing doesn't mean you are paranoid. It means you are choosing to recognize and admit that potential problems could arise at any time.

Finally, the most vital principle when it comes to safety is *confidence*. Having confidence and peace of mind means you have a developed sense of awareness, the right mind-set and are mentally prepared to commit to securing your personal safety on a daily basis.

It is normal for someone to be fearful regarding their personal safety or that of their family, but by taking charge of your safety and making the right decisions, you have a better chance of avoiding danger for you and your family and/or making the right decisions in a potentially dangerous situation.

Developing these core principles will give you a great advantage and allow you to better secure your safety both while traveling and when reaching your destination. It is important to couple these core principles with other basic safety knowledge. Any seasoned criminal will tell you there are certain characteristics they seek in people who appear to be nonthreatening and defenseless. Thankfully, there are things you can do to prevent criminals from selecting you as their next victim.

Strong body language is critical. You are always being watched, so you must appear confident at all times; your body language can reveal your mentality and whether it is negative or positive. It is important to note that it is very easy to retrain the way you carry yourself. You just need to make a conscious effort to present yourself in a certain way, until it becomes second nature. Here are some tips to strengthen the way you use your body language and lessen the likelihood of becoming a victim.

- Focus on the way you walk. Push your shoulders back and lift your head up.
- Walk with confidence and with purpose.
- Stay focused on what is happening around you. Don't be distracted.
- Carry a confident look on your face.
- Don't be afraid to make eye contact if someone looks at you.

These few tips can save your life. Remember that your goal is to not come across as an easy target. With practice, these tips alone will give you more confidence and skills than the majority of the people in this country.

Using your voice is another way to protect against harm. Criminals often test people without them knowing it. For instance, he or she might come up to you and ask you for directions. What appears as an innocent question could actually be a test to determine if you are an easy target—if you are reluctant to answer or speak with a shy voice. You must assess the situation, trust your instincts and determine the appropriate course of action. Do not worry about appearing rude or offensive to someone. Your verbal skills can be used as a weapon. Here are some ways you can use your voice to prevent becoming a victim:

- Learn to say "No!" If you don't know someone and you don't trust their motives, don't be afraid to offend them.
- Stay cool and calm when talking.
- Speak in a clear, even tone, and don't let your voice show fear.

Additionally, what you communicate nonverbally with your eyes and face can also help or hurt you in an emergency situation. You must

- keep your facial expressions straight and calm.
- keep your breathing relaxed and controlled.
- keep your body relaxed.

Your eyes can be trained to see trouble before it happens. You don't have to be paranoid, but anytime you go out in public it would behoove you to be aware of what is going on around you by staying in tune with your environment. Take notice of what people are doing and what their body language is saying to you. These skills will help you stay out of harm's way. The ability to walk and speak with confidence, coupled with seeing potential problems before they happen, deters you from being a target for crime or scam.

Whether you are using verbal or nonverbal language, you must learn to trust your instincts. Fear is real. Listen to what your body is telling you, and be prepared to respond as needed. This is where learning the basics of personal self-defense will prove to be beneficial.

In order to make safety a priority in your life, you have to first admit that your safety is important and then develop the *proper mind-set*. Learn and perfect the basic guidelines stated above. Then by keeping the tips outlined in the remainder of this book fresh in your mind, you will be better equipped to deal with your safety and make the right decisions in the event that you find yourself in a threatening situation.

Chapter Two

Home Safety While You Are Away

How Reliable Is Your Home Security?

How many times have you heard someone use the following statements to describe their thoughts on being safe in the neighborhood they live in? "Things like that don't happen out here in the suburbs, only in the inner city. I don't need an alarm. All I have to do is dial 911 and call the police. They will be here in no time." Another popular remark made, when the security of their home is in doubt, is, "If anyone steps foot in my house while I am here, I'm going to grab my gun and pull a Dirty Harry on them." All of these options would be fine, if they were true, but in reality they are the furthest things from the truth.

The reality about this first fairy tale, "things like this don't happen in the suburbs," is that it is nothing more than a fantasy nurtured by those who believe that their neighborhood is magically shielded from the real world. Today's burglar knows if he is going to risk his freedom and life in order to commit a crime, he'd better make sure the "pot of gold" is worth the risk.

For the most part, expensive homes in the suburbs contain more money, more valuable jewelry, and a slim chance of being caught. In an inner-city environment, people are more aware of crime and spend time finding ways to properly deal with it. If you drive through any crime-ridden neighborhood, you will see bars on the windows and doors to prevent anyone from breaking inside. If someone decides to break in, chances are he will be met with gunfire and possible death. Unless it is a drug-related or planned robbery, most rational people will not take a chance on breaking in with so much opposition. "Smart criminals" know that they must go where there is less opposition and a greater payoff. Most suburbanites are oblivious to this rule which is exactly why their home is a prime target for a break-in. The 911 emergency system is designed to help people, but you first have to call them (assuming you will have the option) and then the police must be dispatched to your house. *How long do you think this will take?* If you are calling the dispatcher as someone is breaking in, *how long do you think it will take a police car to arrive at your house?* Unless they are parked in front of your house, it can take anywhere from seven minutes to a half hour, depending on where they are coming from when the call is received. Nothing against the police, but they can't be everywhere at once. In the real world, smart people won't commit a crime while the police are nearby. Experienced burglars don't want anyone around while they are committing their crimes if they want a successful heist.

Meanwhile, back at your house there is chaos because there was no preset plan to handle this type of emergency. If someone breaks in your house while you are there, either the burglars didn't know you were home, or knew you were home but didn't care. If the latter is the case, you may have more problems than just a burglary. If they are that bold, they either want more (your body, your children, or worse, your life), or they just are not worried about getting caught.

Now as far as pulling a "Dirty Harry" and taking care of business, that isn't as simple as it sounds. From my own experiences with firearms, I know that you must constantly train under stressful situations similar to the way you will have to perform in real life.

This means training in an indoor housing situation much like a home. You will also have to take into consideration where the firearm is at the time of the break-in. Will you be able to reach it in time? How many other people are in the house during the incident? Should you keep the location of the gun to yourself or share with other family members? You are fooling yourself if you think that firing a couple of rounds at some cans in the woods will prepare you for a real home invasion.

If you are not willing to practice and perfect this skill, then do the next best thing: *prepare your family to get out of the house safely.* This will take practice like anything else. You have to practice and simulate what you will do in the event of an actual burglary. Rehearse getting your family out of the house safely and going to a neighbor's house and calling for help. (This is another aspect of crafting a plan. Meet with your neighbors who are within walking distance of your house and discuss how you, as a community, can band together in case of an emergency. Formulate a plan not just as a household but also as a community) Even if you are trained in combat shooting or self-defense training, your goal is to get out alive and uninjured. Don't let your ego get in the way of better judgment. Valuables can be replaced, but not your life or the lives of your family members.

If a burglary happens, it is to the criminal's advantage that the home is empty. If he can find a house where someone is gone for a long period of time, perhaps on vacation, that is the opportune time for him to strike. Your job is to keep the criminal out of the house. How can you do this? Well, one of the first things to do is learn to think like a burglar; ask, *How can I break into my own house?* Then, go about trying to break inside. If you don't think you can do it, have a friend that you trust do it. This way, you can find out where the weaknesses are in your house. Once again, you must think like the criminal.

Burglary is a crime of opportunity. Even a decent criminal knows to case an area to find an easy target. They determine who is frequently in and out of their house, and his or her schedule. Criminals look for a house with easy access into and out of the neighborhood. They want a big payoff with the least amount of trouble. Most break-ins will occur during the day while people are at work. Most evening burglaries happen when people are gone for a length of time or the home is simply unoccupied. These types of crimes are committed quickly. The criminal wants to get in and out for petty cash or small things that can be sold rapidly.

Then there is the other possibility: a burglar who gets wind of a family going on vacation. They live in a beautiful house, in a nice part of the suburbs, surrounded by woods for seclusion. This is the ideal burglary: perfect opportunity, unlimited amount of time, with no one around to stop them. The criminal gets a truck, gets a couple of his trusted buddies, and proceeds to clear the house out. As he's moving out the last of the haul, he realizes how easy this was compared to breaking inside a more modest home. There was an alarm, but it wasn't on; the side door to the garage was unlocked, so he didn't even have to break in. Like most people who are always in a rush, this family left many valuable items out in the open, making them easy to find. Strangely, they did have a safe, but did not put anything of real value inside (or they filled it with valuables and left it unlocked)! These victims made it so easy, just like most Americans who are creatures of habit.

The burglars are able to take their time loading up the truck with several big-screen TVs, computers, appliances, jewelry, important documents and papers, and much more. They even take the time to fix themselves sandwiches and drinks. It is a bold robbery, but they did their homework and knew the situation was in their favor.

This is a true story that happened to someone I know. I didn't use names or the place, but no need; break-ins like these occur every day.

Percentage-wise, wealthier people tend to be more careless when it comes to any type of security, especially that of their homes. I cannot count how many times I've watched the news and seen a report about a string of burglaries in an upper income neighborhood, where nine out of ten times the criminal didn't even have to break in. All he had to do was open an unlocked door and walk inside. This is scary, but it happens all the time.

People who live in the upper-middle income brackets and above tend to not think about crime in the same way as those in the lower half. They are aware of crime and realize it is going on, but as they say, out of sight is out of mind.

So what can you really do? If you cannot answer this question, like most people you will feel lost, and you deal with the situation by pretending that it will never happen and hope you will never have to deal with burglary. But that won't work.

You *must* first face reality and admit there is a problem. You *can* handle this, if you take the time to learn the basics of home security and how not to become a victim. Remember: make it difficult for a burglar to break inside your house (this will be discussed further in the next chapter). You want him to think twice, if he is considering, and put up enough barriers and deterrents in your home-security plan that it would just be too much of a chance for him to take. In the end, all you want is "peace of mind."

According to Robert Young Pelton's book, *The World's Most Dangerous Places*, a survey was given to vacationers in Europe and surprising information was noted about them. Here is the order in which vacationers worried about things when on vacation:

Worry	**Percentage (%)**
1. Burglary of home while away	90
2. Illness and accidents on holiday	40
3. Family Safety	33
4. Poor Accommodations	26
5. Bad Weather	19
6. Bad Food	18
7. Work	6

This is a very surprising thing to learn about people who are supposed to be on vacation for rest and relaxation. You leave home to get away from everything for a while. As you lie on the beach somewhere, trying to relax, you are worried about the house—whether you turned off the stove, or locked the front door before you left. But that's not the real reason you're anxious. The reason is there was no in-depth preparation or planning before leaving for vacation. When you plan for something and realistically deal with it, you have a better chance of taking care of the circumstances. In this case, by taking a look at how to make your house more secure and safer, it will give you greater peace of mind while you are away on vacation. Peace of mind means rest and happiness. Why would you want to be on vacation and worry about something you could have prevented? *Make sure your house is a hard place to break into.*

Some habits are hard to break. But think about the alternative—you would really feel badly if someone broke into your house and harmed you or a loved one, when you could have prevented it with minor adjustments to the security of your home.

Don't put off this important decision to make your home a safe haven for you and your family. Just a few adjustments can make the difference between life and death and give you peace of mind when you do travel or go on vacation.

Chapter Three

Pretravel Safety

Unfortunately, your home is the most vulnerable when no one is there. When an intruder finds out that you and your family will be going away on vacation, it's like hitting the jackpot. The best way to prevent a burglary would be to keep your travel plans as private as possible. Take special precautions to increase the security of your home by installing a superb alarm system, and follow these simple but important pretravel safety tips. They will give you peace of mind and enable you to better enjoy your trip. At the same time, you will be making it more difficult for the bad guys to break into your home, and they will move on to seek an easier target.

A. Ensure your home looks lived in while you are away on a trip

1. Depending on the length of your trip, stop the delivery of your newspaper and mail service or arrange to have a trusted friend, neighbor, or relative pick it up on a daily

basis. Whomever you choose, make sure it is someone you don't mind seeing what is in your mail.
2. Have the grass cut or the snow shoveled while you are away. This is a judgment call depending on how long you will be away and how fast your grass grows.
3. Set up timers on different appliances to turn on/off at different times of the day or night. You don't want to overdo this, as there is always the possibility of fire. Your best bet is to setup your computer or stereo to play music at different times of the day or night. There are different kinds of software to help you do this (Music Matchbox, etc.).
4. Have a trusted friend, neighbor, or relative check on your house, or stay in it, while you are away. The key word here is *trust*.

B. What to do a week prior to the trip

1. Make a list of things you need to do and things you need to take (take the time frame into consideration and come up with a game plan).
2. Make sure to pay all of your important bills.
3. Ensure that all your insurance policies are up to date such as home, life, and, car. Check to make sure the insurance covers all of your health needs, especially when traveling out of the country. Certain insurances will not cover you if you leave the country, and you may have to consider additional insurance.
4. Call the hotel where you will stay to confirm your reservations and inquire about the important details associated with your stay, such as transportation options in the area, hotel security, and the nearest hospital.
5. If traveling out of the country, you will need a valid passport and, in most countries, a visa. When you are traveling on business, a business visa should be obtained; otherwise, a tourist visa is acceptable.
6. Be sure all of your immunization shots are up to date.
7. When bringing electronics of any kind, make it a point to buy a universal AC converter and adapter kit or check to

see if the country you are visiting has compatible outlets for U.S. products.

C. What to do the day before the trip

1. Confirm plane, hotel, and car reservations.
2. Make a detailed list of everything you plan to take with you and follow the list when you start packing.
3. Pack as light as possible. Don't bring just expensive clothes and jewelry.
4. Double check that a trusted friend, neighbor, or relative has all of your flight and hotel information, as well as all of the appropriate numbers and a detailed itinerary.
5. If you have medication you must take, be sure to pack enough for the entire trip. Keep it with your carry-on luggage, so it will be with you at all times. Also, keep all medications in its original packaging to avoid security problems.
6. Keep all your home documents in order. Make sure there are copies of your insurance policies and wills which are accessible, so that if anything happens to you while you were away, your loved ones will be able to resolve matters easily.

D. What to do on the day of the trip

1. Plan to leave early.
2. Have a backup plan in case your ride is late or you have car problems.
3. Double check your packing list to ensure you have packed everything you need.
4. Gather all your important papers and personal items in a carry-on bag and keep it with you at all times.
5. Only carry as much cash or as many credits cards as absolutely necessary.
6. Make sure all electronics are unplugged (with the exception of the ones you plan to use on timers) and that windows and doors are locked in your home.

E. Have a game plan for keeping your money safe

1. Only carry as much money as you need.
2. If you have to carry a large amount of money, do not carry it all together. Hide it on different places on your body, or consider travelers checks.
3. Never flash large amounts of money in public, as someone is always watching.
4. Pay for big-ticket items on your credit card to ensure that you have proof of purchase in the event that something goes wrong with your goods or services.
5. Make sure you get your credit card back at the end of each transaction.
6. Always keep your credit cards with you. Never leave your cards in your car, hotel room, etc.
7. If your credit card is lost or stolen, be sure to report it right away.

Keeping Your Home Safe While You Are Away

If you have no one to watch over your home while you are away, here are a few tips that can help keep your house safe. You must first start thinking like a thief who is breaking into your house. You must *case out* your home, at day and at night, looking for ways to get in. You will be surprised how easy it can be to break in. Is the latch on the backyard gate rusty and easily bypassed? Are first-floor bedroom windows low enough to crawl through? Your job is to make it so hard for a criminal to break-in that he would rather skip your house, and take his chances with an easier pick somewhere else.

Outside Security

1. Provide sufficient lighting at all doors and windows.
2. Keep the bushes, trees, and shrubbery cut down so burglars cannot use them to hide.
3. A large dog can be a great security weapon as a warning device and a deterrent. The dog shouldn't be trained to

attack, because when you travel, it may be hard to find someone to stop by to feed him/her.
4. If you have a second car, arrange to have it moved occasionally in your absence. This will appear as if someone is home.
5. Use exterior alarm signs as a deterrent.

Inside Security

1. Exterior doors should be locked at all times.
2. Every outside door should come equipped with deadbolt locks.
3. You should have strong doors with reinforced doorframes to keep the door closed shut in the event someone tries to force his way in.
4. Patio and sliding doors should be secured with vertical bolt locks and shatterproof glass. Also place a sawed-off broomstick in the door track to serve as extra security for the door.
5. Make sure that the garage door is secured with locks on each side of the door.
6. Doors of attached garages should be secured with deadbolt locks.
7. The garage door should be secured as best as possible; if thieves get inside, it will be easier to break into the house because they are undercover.
8. Lock the garage and turn off the automatic garage door opener, if you are to be away for any length of time.
9. Make sure that all windows are equipped with strong locking devices.
10. Window unit air conditioners should be anchored down securely, to prevent someone from coming through the opening.
11. If you don't have an alarm system, get one. If a burglar gets inside, the sound of the alarm may be your last line of defense.

12. To protect anything of value, you should store it inside a safe. Even better, sign up for a safe deposit box at your bank in case there is a fire.
13. Inform the police in your neighborhood that you will be gone. They will come by and check on your house every day.
14. Stop all deliveries such as the mail and newspapers.
15. Use several timers throughout the house to turn the lights off and on at different times of day.
16. Be sure to leave an itinerary with someone, so that you can be notified in case of an emergency.
17. Get to know your neighbors. They are more likely to let you know something suspicious is going on around your property and will call for help.
18. Avoid publicity about your trip.
19. Make sure to double check everything and lock up before you leave.

Any business or pleasure trips that you take should be positive experiences. The last thing you want to find when you return is that your personal property has been tampered with or stolen; worse is finding out you could have prevented it by taking some of the precautions in this book.

Take some time now to choose five ways you can make your home more secure while you are away.

1.

2.

3.

4.

5.

Chapter Four

Car Safety on the Road

Each mode of transportation has its own safety concerns. When traveling by car, for instance, you can be faced with problems with your vehicle, other drivers, being pulled over by police, carjacking, and more. While some of these seem like routine encounters, they can lead to dangerous situations. What if your car ran out of gas in a bad neighborhood? What if another driver purposely caused an accident on a deserted road in an effort to attack you? What if you were pulled over by a phony police officer? What if you were carjacked and no one was around to help?

The best thing you can do is be prepared—do what you can to prevent potentially harmful situations, and have knowledge of what should and should not be done in certain situations.

Regardless of the reasons for your trip, it is important to always remember the following rules before you hit the road:

- Make sure your car is always properly maintained (and have it tuned up, if you have not done so in a while).
- Check tire pressure on all wheels and make sure the spare is in good condition.
- Keep the battery charged
- Have a car emergency kit.
- Carry a cell phone.
- Remember to always keep the gas tank at least one-quarter of the way full.
- Never pick up hitchhikers.

- Always keep your doors locked, whether you are in or out of the car (even if you are just going to pay for gas or run into the store) and never leave your car running.
- Always tell a family member or friend your travel plans and either have someone meet you at your destination or plan on calling a shuttle, or catching a cab, to reach your destination.
- Try to avoid looking like you are a tourist on vacation.
- Know how to get to and from your destination. This means plan ahead.
- When lost and in need of directions, go to a gas station or a convenience store or ask a police officer if you can find one. If you must ask a stranger, do so in a well-populated area.
- Keep the car windows up, especially when you are driving in a major metropolitan area.
- Always leave your luggage or packages in your trunk.
- When highway driving, remember to plan your trip. Always stay focused and alert while driving. If you are traveling a long distance, take a fifteen-minute break every hour to stay mentally fresh.
- If possible, never take out a road map in public.
- Try to avoid traveling alone.
- If someone tailgates you, stay cool and let the person go around you. Never provoke or be provoked by a motorist on the road.

Safety tips in the event of car troubles are as follows:

- At the first sign of trouble, get out of traffic. Pull over as soon as possible onto the shoulder, and turn on your emergency blinkers.
- Use your cell phone to call for assistance. If no cell phone is accessible, try coasting along the shoulder of the road until you reach one of the roadside assistance phones located on most major highways.
- Tie a white towel on your antenna, or if you have a "Call Police" sign, place it in the window.
- If you have flares and reflectors, put those several feet behind the car and keep a flashlight and first aid kit handy. Watch out for drivers who are not paying attention.
- If a stranger stops by to help you, crack open the window and thank him but tell him you would prefer that he would call the police. If you are a woman traveling alone, you can also say, "Thank you! My boyfriend went to call for help. However, I would appreciate you also placing a call for me."
- If you call for a tow truck, make sure it is a legitimate by checking for flashing lights and the proper markings.

Avoiding a Carjacking

You are at your weakest when entering and exiting your vehicle. These are times you normally have your keys accessible and are preoccupied with other thoughts. When you are getting in and out of your car, survey the area and stay in tune with your surroundings. Always keep your windows up and doors locked.

Carjackers are often looking for cars that are already running, so make sure to keep the doors locked while the vehicle is running. Get in and out of the car as quickly as possible. If you have children, put them in their car seats and then go around and get in the car and lock it, before taking the time to buckle them in. When approaching a stop sign or stoplight, always leave ample space between your car and the car in front of

How To Vacation & Travel Safely

you. This will allow you the needed space to drive away if an attacker approaches your car. We are often conditioned to do what is right, but if you are stopped and someone approaches your car, do what is necessary to get away, even if that means running a red light. While at a stop sign or stoplight, do not put on makeup, read, balance your checkbook, or anything that will take your attention away from your surroundings. Stay focused on what is going on around you. Always look in the rearview mirror.

Be sensible. If a carjacker is in control, be rational and give them what they want. Your car is replaceable, but your life isn't. Be aware that carjackers are not interested in harming your children. Talk calmly and explain that you have a child in the car, and they can have the vehicle but you *must* get your child. *Never leave with a carjacker.*

Also, be aware of the "bump and rob" technique, where carjackers purposely hit you; when you get out to determine the damage, they carjack (this often occurs in isolated areas).

If you are involved in an accident, keep the following tips in mind:

- Make sure you aren't seriously injured.
- If you have a cell phone, immediately call the police.
- If anyone is hurt, perform first aid, but don't move the victim.
- If someone looks as if they are seriously injured but claim to be okay, call an ambulance anyway.
- Warn oncoming vehicles of the accident with flares or reflectors.
- Gather insurance information from each other. Never admit guilt.
- If there are any witnesses to the accident, obtain their names and phone numbers.
- Write down any details about the accident that you can remember, including if it is raining, who had the right of way, etc.

- Consider carrying a portable camera, or use the camera on your phone, if you have one.
- After a police report is made, obtain that information to give to your insurance company right away.

Believe it or not, criminals have been known to pose as police officers in an attempt to lure you. To prevent falling victim to this trick, make sure to check out the police car by looking for identifiable markings. Remember, you have the right to request identification from a police officer who is not in uniform. Always keep your door locked and just crack your window. If you don't feel comfortable and believe you are in a phony situation, request that you go to a public place to deal with the situation. If it is a real officer, they will understand your concern and react appropriately.

Car Safety Tips When You Are Traveling Abroad

- Know where you are going ahead of time. Most people will be nice and try to help you, but if you ask the wrong person for directions, he or she can send you to the wrong place and set you up for a robbery.
- As you are driving, keep the doors locked and wear your seat belt at all times.
- Avoid driving at night when possible.
- Don't leave valuables in your car. If you must leave items of value in your car, keep them out of sight or in the trunk.
- If at all possible, don't park your car on the street. Try to park it in a garage or another secure place.
- Never pick up hitchhikers.
- Never get out of the car if something looks suspicious. If things don't look right, trust your instincts and drive away.

One of the greatest technologies for vehicle safety is the OnStar in-vehicle security system. OnStar was created to help protect you and your family while driving. They offer emergency services like twenty-four-hour access to advisers for your help, and roadside emergency assistance. Among the other services they provide are tracking your car down if it is stolen, or opening your car if the keys get locked inside. The service does charge a fee, but it is invaluable if you travel frequently.

Dealing with Road Rage

The problem with crime is that it can happen anytime or anywhere on our vast highways or city streets, and road rage has become an ongoing problem over the last decade. It happens when one driver gets mad at another driver and attempts to retaliate with anything from verbal assault to physical violence. This situation can be brought on by a million reasons, but two of the most common reasons are cutting someone off, and not letting someone pass when you are driving too slow in the passing lane. Whatever the reason, this is a very dangerous problem, and people have been killed because of it.

No one benefits from a road rage incident. If you ever find yourself in a situation where anger is overtaking you while you are driving, take a deep breath, relax, and pull over if you have to.

Some tips to minimize your chances of becoming a victim of road rage are as follows:

- If someone attempts to run you off the road, you should slow down and try to stay calm. The worst thing you can do is to try and outrun the other driver. If you drive slowly, this will make it more difficult for the other driver to run you off the road or cause you to have an accident.
- Your goal should be to drive to a populated area, and if you can, memorize the license plate number of the other vehicle (window notepads always come in handy). Don't ever drive home. Try to look for safe places to go: fire departments, police stations, or hospitals. As soon as

possible, call 911 on your cell phone, and let the police know what is going on and where you are attempting to go for safety.
- If you are cornered and cannot drive away, your first response to an enraged driver should be to try to calm the situation down. Do not get out of the car. Lock your doors, crack the window, and try to apologize. If you start to argue with the other driver, this may only escalate the situation. Just try to buy as much time as possible. If you cannot drive away from the situation, don't get out of the car; stall for time. If the other driver cannot get to you, they will most likely cool down and leave in disgust. For the most part, this situation happens because the driver is already upset or angry at someone or something else, and you simply provided an outlet for him or her to express their anger.

Take some time now to choose five ways you can make your road trip safer.

1.

2.

3.

4.

5.

Chapter Five

Bus and Train Safety

Why do people travel by train or bus? Some say it is a cheaper way to travel; others may be fed up with the headaches and worries associated with going to the airport and flying. You can leave the driving to someone else and not have to put up with the hassles of waiting in long lines, embarrassing pat downs, and taking a chance that you were overbooked on a crowded flight and getting bumped.

Others may love this form of travel because you can enjoy the scenery; or, when not in a big hurry, buses or trains can be a more relaxing way to travel. It is also a great time to read a book or get work done on your computer.

Now let's look at the other side of the coin. Just like an airport, when you go to a bus or train terminal, there will be plenty of people. The only difference is no one has to go through a security check. There may be a few security guards standing around, but they can't see everything or be everywhere at once. This means people can do or bring anything they would like once they are onboard.

Staying Safe in a Bus or Train Terminal

For the most part, many crimes committed happen in the terminal. These crimes can range from a variety of scams, pickpocketings, and purse snatchings to rapes, robberies, and killings. Most of your worst crimes happen outside the terminal or in the restrooms. So the key here is to stay alert and focused. Keep your distance from strangers. This may sound rude, but don't start any unnecessary conversations with or buy anything from strangers. If you are approached and don't feel comfortable about the situation, be confident and use good eye contact; tell them that you can't help them or you are not interested. Again, this may sound rude but is better to be safe than sorry.

Another situation in which you must be alert is while waiting for your transportation. If you can get a seat against the wall, this is best. If not, you should stand against the wall or a corner. Keep your belongings in your sight at all times, including watching your purse, briefcase, or laptops. If you are going to spend several hours in a train or a bus station, put your belongings in a coin locker. If there are no lockers, and you are alone, the next best thing is to find a seat around other people and place your valuables between your legs. Just in case you fall asleep, keep your tickets and all valuables close to your body. Women should have a shoulder bag with heavy straps. This makes it difficult for a thief to grab your bag and run.

Once it is time to board the train or bus, be careful and alert as you stand in line. Remember, keep your business from strangers, and don't let them lead you into unnecessary conversations.

Train and Bus Smarts

- Dress comfortably and low-key. Don't wear clothes or jewelry that will attract attention.
- Travel light and never carry expensive luggage. Nice luggage attracts thieves, and traveling light lessens the chances of being bogged-down and vulnerable.

- If possible, check unneeded baggage under the bus in storage or, if you are on a train, in the baggage car.
- Any luggage to be carried on should be kept with you at all times. If you must leave your seat, you should either take it with you or secure it to your seat with a strong cable lock.
- If you are on a bus, sit where you will feel comfortable, but always stay in sight of the driver.
- On a train, choose a compartment that is carrying the most people, and sit with those you feel most comfortable.
- If you have a private compartment, keep the door locked and identify anyone wishing to come inside.
- Don't choose the window seat as you may be "blocked in" by a potential assailant. Always choose an aisle seat for quick exit.

The key to your safety in this type of situation is to stay alert and be low-key.

Take time now to choose three ways you can make your train or bus trip safe:

1.

2.

3.

Chapter Six

Airport Safety

Traveling by plane has changed a lot over the past ten years. If you don't have the patience, this process can drive you crazy. Long lines, higher ticket prices, and fewer planes (that are normally late) can make you less likely to want to fly if you find these challenges frustrating. In addition, there is now the added stress of stricter security that takes place when you go through the security checkpoints and screening process. You may be poked, prodded, and pat down after you go through the metal detector. If you set off the alarm, you will subjected to an even stricter search, and if they don't like what they see or hear, get ready for a long night at the airport being interrogated.

Airport security does not play games in this post-9/11 era, so it would be to your advantage to make going to the airport a positive and serious situation. If airport security requests information from you, then you need to have the right answers and the proper documentation if you don't want to miss your flight. If airport security isn't satisfied with what they hear or see,

How To Vacation & Travel Safely

you can be detained. 9/11 changed everything when it comes to traveling by plane, and you can be sure that the security won't lessen anytime soon.

If you have traveled by plane long enough, then you know there will be some headaches associated with flying, but also remember that these delays are for the benefit of your safety and the safety of your loved ones. The following tips will educate you on how to deal with the process of this sometimes stressful event.

What to Do When You Reach the Airport

1. No matter how you travel to the airport, be sure to arrive no later than one hour before your plane leaves. During the busy times of the year or holidays, two hours before takeoff is a must.
2. If you have purchased your ticket early, you can check-in your baggage at the curb outside the terminal. This can save you the time and hassle of waiting in long lines. The skycap issues boarding passes, so once you have checked your bags, you can head directly to your gate for check-in.
3. Get to the gate and check-in as soon as possible. Anything can happen to delay you, including cancellations, getting bumped, etc. In the event something does change, you are giving yourself enough time to make the necessary changes.
4. Since 9/11, the airlines have become very strict about what can be carried onto the plane. Knives, scissors, needles, or any other sharp objects cannot be packed into your carry-on luggage. They must go into your checked luggage. Firearms must be checked in at the counter and then stored in your luggage. Certain items such as flammable materials, fireworks, or flares are prohibited.
5. Make sure to take everything out of your pockets or off your body that is metal, because it will set off the metal detector. This can be an inconvenience and cause an unnecessary search.

6. While you are going through the metal detector, keep an eye on personal items as they are put through the X-ray machine. This is the best time for someone to steal your possessions from the conveyor belt if you are not paying attention.
7. Beware of con men or women who will create a distraction to pick your pocket, or while someone else takes off with your bags.
8. You also have to be cautious when using public restrooms. For better protection, use a stall at the far end next to the wall. Don't hang anything on the hook or set anything of value on the floor near the door. Someone can reach over or under and snatch your valuables. Keep them on your lap or close to the wall, so that they can't be grabbed.
9. Never carry a stranger's bags, and don't ask a stranger to watch yours.
10. Stay alert. This is the best rule you can go by.

While on the Plane

1. Place your carry-on items in an overhead bin across the aisle, rather than over your head, so that you can keep an eye on them.
2. Listen to the safety announcements and familiarize yourself with the life vest and oxygen mask. Check out the safety card in the seat pocket.
3. Always keep your seatbelt buckled while you are seated. This will protect you from any sudden turbulence.
4. Keep an eye on passengers that act suspiciously. 9/11 taught us that alert passengers make a difference when it comes to minimizing the damage terrorists can inflict on those on the ground.

Air Rage

On the flip side of the coin, even with most stringent security checks, there might be some potentially violent and disruptive passengers who slip through the screening process. If a person shows aggressive behavior due to drunkenness or mental instability, the flight crew has been trained to handle what we call *air rage*. It won't take long to identify a passenger who can be a potential problem. If you feel a passenger can become a threat, discreetly notify a member of the flight crew.

You should never try to handle a problem passenger by yourself, but if a situation gets too far out of hand with a truly violent person as the flight crew is trying to restrain him or her, you could very well be called upon to give a helping hand. When your safety and that of the passengers is in jeopardy, you must do whatever possible to help.

Hijacking/Hostage Situations

According to the Web site www.travel.state.gov, while every hostage situation is different, certain considerations are important.

"The U.S. government policy is firm. We will negotiate, but not make concessions to terrorists. To do so would only increase the risk of further hostage incidents. When Americans are abducted overseas, we look to the host government to exercise its responsibility under international law to protect all persons within its territories and to bring about the safe release of hostages. We work closely with these governments from the outset of a hostage incident to ensure that our citizens and other innocent victims are released as quickly and safely as possible."

Normally, the most dangerous phases of a hijacking or hostage situation are the beginning, and if there is a rescue attempt, the end. At the outset, the terrorists typically are tense, high strung, and may behave irrationally. It is extremely important that you remain calm and alert during this time and manage your own behavior. Avoid resistance and sudden or threatening movements. Do not struggle or try to escape until you are certain of being successful.

If You Are Hijacked

1. Make a concerted effort to relax. Prepare yourself mentally, physically, and emotionally for the possibility of a long ordeal.

2. Try to remain inconspicuous; avoid direct eye contact and the appearance of observing your captors' actions.
3. Avoid alcoholic beverages. Consume little food and water.
4. Consciously put yourself in a mode of passive cooperation. Talk normally. Do not complain, avoid belligerency, and comply with all the orders and instructions.
5. If questioned, keep your answers short. Don't volunteer information or make unnecessary remarks.
6. Don't try to be a hero, endangering yourself and others.
7. Maintain your sense of personal dignity and gradually increase your requests for personal comforts. Make these requests in a reasonable low-key manner.
8. If you are involved in a lengthier drawn-out situation, try to establish a rapport with your captors, avoiding political discussions or other confrontational subjects.
9. Think positively. Avoid a sense of despair. Rely on your inner resource. Remember that you are a valuable commodity to your captors. It is important to them to keep you alive and well.

How Would You Handle a Hijacking?

These rules were made before the horrific tragedy of 9/11. Since this unthinkable tragedy has happened, the rules have changed and so have people's perceptions of how to respond. Here is the reality of the situation. Security at airports and on planes has increased and remains at an all-time high. The chances of another tragedy like 9/11 would be very unlikely, but not impossible. Once the security at the airports becomes relaxed, the chances of someone pulling off a hijacking will increase.

Here is some positive information to make us feel good as we fly the friendly skies:

Besides the increased security at the airports as you make your way to the plane, there has been increased training for the pilots and crew members. In addition to the self-defense training the crew has gone through, there are also laws being passed to allow them to carry guns in the cockpit. The government has trained and placed sky marshals on every flight. Their job is to defend against hijackings and terrorist attacks such as those that occurred on 9/11.

With all the good intentions, however this program has had its problems. Besides being understaffed and overworked, there still isn't enough money for the program to be successful. According to the Center for Defense Information (CDI) fact sheet, there have been management problems, exhaustive work schedules, and too many other problems to get into, but the one single thing that is most disturbing is that air marshals can only be on 50 percent of the flights and concentrate on the nation's twenty-five most high-risk airports. Things are better, but by no means are they perfect.

So, would you completely depend on the flight crew or an air marshal, if you were unfortunate enough to be on a plane that was being hijacked? I wouldn't. The crew may be trained, and the air marshal may or may not be onboard to help thwart the attack, but when it is all said and done, if you want to come out of the situation alive, you will have a better chance if you have mentally and physically dealt with the situation ahead of time.

Play the game of "what if?" What would I do if the plane were taken over? Have you ever taken the time to think about how you would handle a situation of this magnitude? Do you work out or have you ever taken a self-defense class? It's not healthy to go around being worried or thinking about things that haven't happened yet, but it is smart to be prepared for something as important as this. There are no guarantees, but if a situation like this were to occur, I would rather take my chances and deal with the problem at hand than to just stand by and do nothing. If I were going to die, I would rather go out fighting.

According to most of the people I've spoken to, as well as people on the radio and TV, they for the most part feel the same way. Since 9/11, the rules have changed. People will not sit by, let someone threaten them on a plane, and not do anything. Most of them will not be trained but will still attempt to do something to thwart the attack. You just have to roll the dice and wish for the best.

This is a very unpleasant thing to think about, but since 9/11, this could be the number one fear for people who use planes to travel. The best way to deal with these worries is to get some self-defense training and then make a mental plan of how to deal with the situation.

Reaching Your Destination and Beyond

1. Make sure you get the right carry-on luggage before you leave the plane.
2. Once you exit the plane, you should go immediately to the baggage claim area. A thief could beat you to the claim area and steal your luggage. These days, because of the cost, many airports don't even bother to check the claim tickets.
3. Unfortunately, many bags look alike. You should already have a personal ID tag on all of your checked bags so that you can get the correct luggage. Tying a familiar colored ribbon on the bag will help distinguish yours from the rest.
4. Always check your bags to make sure they have not been tampered with. If they have, or if any luggage is missing, immediately go to the airline baggage claim office and file a report. They will usually have you fill out a claims form. If any of your luggage is missing and is not found, or if anything is stolen, then you are entitled to compensation. They normally can locate lost luggage within twenty-four to forty-eight hours, and will have it delivered to you.

Take some time now to choose three ways you can make your plane trip safe:

1.

2.

3.

Chapter Seven

Safely Getting to Your Destination

Before you reach your destination, you should already know how you intend to reach either your hotel, cruise ship, or any other vacation spot. Most large hotels have shuttle buses that will take their guests back and forth to the airport. Most people are satisfied with this type of transportation, but if you are traveling for business or need a car to get around during your vacation, you will need other forms of transportation.

The most common forms of transportation going to and from most large airports are taxicabs, metrolinks, or subways. Whenever you use commercial transportation, there are certain rules you must abide by to ensure that you get to your destination safely.

Taxi Safety

Taxicabs are the most common way to travel from the airport, but not all cabdrivers can be trusted. Unfortunately, anyone can get a car and dress it up to look like a taxi. There are so-called gypsy cabdrivers who are legitimate, but there is no way of knowing who is and who isn't. At airports or other places with taxi stands, only authorized taxicabs are used. If you are still not sure, ask an airport transportation employee or a hotel doorman.

Here are some tips to ensure a safe trip to and from the airport if you take a cab:

- Make sure you choose the cab rather than the cabdriver choosing you. Don't just get into a cab because it's the first one you see. Read the cab markings on the outside to make sure it has the same markings as some of the other cabs in line. Can you see the ID card in front of the cab? Does the driver have a two-way radio and meter? If it doesn't at least have these things, something isn't right. If it doesn't feel right, get the next cab.
- Ask a staff member from either the airport or the hotel how much it will cost to take a cab to a certain destination. If you are going to your hotel, there is usually a set price.
- The other thing you must think about is sharing a cab with someone. If you don't know the person or persons, you could be taking a chance of being set up. If you do share, make sure they are going to the same destination. The problem is, if the other passengers get out before you, they can just as easily take one of your bags with theirs. Sometimes the cabdriver and the passenger can be working together.
- Keep your luggage with you. This will give you a better chance of keeping an eye on it, and if there is a dispute over pricing or you don't trust the situation, you can leave much easier. Only let the driver put your luggage in the trunk if there isn't room for them inside.
- The best place to sit in a cab is the back seat, directly behind the driver. You are at a better vantage point if

the driver isn't on the up "up and up." He will have to stop the car and turn around if he plans to do anything. This will also give you more time to react should there be a problem.
- There have been some instances where people taking cabs have been dropped off at a different place than where they wanted to go and were robbed. It is a good idea to find out how far your destination is from the airport. Also, as you may know, some drivers take an unsuspecting passenger the long way to his destination, so that they can charge him or her more cab fare.
- Always keep a cell phone with you.

Most cabdrivers are honest and trustworthy. They want to serve the customer to the best of his or her ability. However, there are a few bad cabdrivers out there giving a bad name to the honest ones. Remember, the key here is to assess and handle the situation before you get into the cab.

Take some time now and choose three ways you can make your cab ride safe:

1.

2.

3.

MetroLink (Light Rail) and Subway

The light rail system (MetroLink) and the subway are basically the same mode of transportation, except the light rail system goes under and above the ground, while the subway runs mainly underground. While millions of people ride this form of transportation every day, the underground terminals and rail cars are a criminal's paradise. When the terminals become crowded, this is the best time for pickpockets and thieves to do their work. Remember, never look like a tourist. Fit in and be alert. You must keep your valuables close to you, and keep your money well hidden and hard to get. Also, remember to walk and talk in a confident way. There will be times when a thief may first try to talk to you, or even try to intimidate you, but you will need to stay strong. If someone tries to do anything like that, you must stand strong; have good eye contact and use a positive, strong voice.

Here are a few tips to stay safe in a subway terminal and in a rail car:

- When waiting for the subway, stand as far back from the edge as you can. Mistakes can happen, and you could fall or be pushed if you stand too close to the edge.
- Experienced pickpockets can pick out a tourist in the crowd. You must keep your purse close, and if carrying a wallet, keep it in an inside pocket on your body. Consider having two wallets: one with a little money to give away if confronted and another that contains your most important items such as your license, credit cards, etc.
- When you are going to sit down, your seat must be chosen with safety in mind. *Never* ride in an empty car. If you find yourself alone, simply exit to the next one. Generally, the center cars on the trains get the heavier traffic. Remember, there is safety in numbers.
- Avoid constantly referring to the subway map on the subway or metro rail. This will advertise that you are not sure where you are going.
- Remember to dress low-key, and leave the expensive jewelry at home.
- Don't sit near the door, because a thief can snatch your belongings and run off.
- When getting off the subway, stay focused and be alert. Make sure to scan the area to see if anyone makes you feel uncomfortable. *If you don't like what you see, don't get out.* Most pickpockets like to take people's belongings while everyone is standing at the exit.

Pick three ways you can make your subway or MetroLink ride safer.

1.

2.

3.

Picking up Your Rental Vehicle

Make sure there is nothing that will give away the fact that you are driving a rental vehicle. This is a sure way to tell the bad guys you are from out of town. Any smart criminal knows, if you are from out of town, there is a good chance you are carrying money and other things of value. There is also a good chance you may not know how to get to your destination right away.

Keep maps, brochures, tickets, etc., in the glove compartments or purse. When you take out a map to read it, unfold it in your lap, not up high in the window. Minimize the appearance that you are a traveler. If you have anything of value like your luggage in your car, you should keep it in the trunk so as not to tip off anyone who sees it in your vehicle that you are traveling and from out of town.

Keep your doors locked and windows up. This will prevent criminals from reaching in and stealing something of value and keep the bad guys out of your vehicle. *Never* pick up hitchhikers. Keep a cell phone with you in case of an emergency, and make sure that you have the directions to your destination before you leave the rental car dealer. *Don't* look like a tourist.

Take some time now to choose three ways you can be safer in your rental car.

1.

2.

3.

Chapter Eight

Hotel and Motel Safety

Once you get to your hotel or motel, take the first twenty seconds to look at everything from a safety perspective. If you drove yourself there, here are some questions you should ask yourself:

- How is the security on the parking lot?
- Is the parking lot well lit?
- How far is the parking lot from the entrance?
- Is valet parking offered?
- How is the hotel security?

Precautions to Take Once Inside the Hotel

1. Register with first initial and last name only. Never register as "Miss" or "Mrs."
2. Protect your room number information. Ask the clerk not to announce your number when you are registering.

3. Try to get a room near the elevator but not right next to it. Avoid rooms that are down long hallways or next to stairways.
4. Ask what the fire alarm sounds like. Most people will ignore the alarm because they don't know what it sounds like.
5. If your room does not have a safe, you may need to use the hotel safe to store any valuables you may have, but wait until you get to your room and call about this information.
6. Never invite someone you have just met to your room or give them your room number.

Elevator Safety

Unless it is an emergency, never take the stairs. You could be isolating yourself to danger if you do. However, even though the elevator is there to make your life easier, you still have to use it with caution.

- Never get on an elevator if you feel uncomfortable, or you don't like what you see before you go in.
- If someone boards the elevator while you are on it and you feel uneasy, get off before the door closes or press the button for the next floor and get off.
- If for some reason while you're on the elevator, someone is acting strange, get to the control panel and start pushing as many buttons as possible.

Room Security

When going to your room, especially if you are by yourself, be cautious of what is going on around you. You could be a victim of a push-in crime. This is when a guest is opening the door to his or her room and someone sneaks up from behind and pushes the guest into the room. If you don't feel comfortable going into your room for whatever reason, don't be afraid to go back to the front desk and state your feeling and ask for help.

Here are some tips to insure your room safety:

- Door keys: the better hotels use electronic strip cards, which can be reprogrammed after each guest checks out.
- Once inside, keep the deadbolt locked. Most hotel doors have peepholes. Don't ever open the door for anyone unless you know who it is.
- Make sure all windows and balcony doors are locked regardless of what floor you are staying on. If you have a door to the adjoining room, make sure it is locked.
- Make sure your phone is in good working order.
- Be aware of a popular hotel scam where you will get a call from the front desk to verify your credit card number and expiration date. Like most people, you give them the information without much thought. Later on when you get your credit card statement, you find charges you never made. Only then do you realize you gave your credit card number to the wrong person.
- Never open the door for someone just because they say they work for the hotel and are coming to check on something, i.e., the smoke alarm. Announce that you are calling down to the front desk to verify their claims.
- If you are going to the vending machine just for a minute, don't prop your door open. This will make it easy for someone to sneak in and wait for you.
- If you travel a lot, you should consider purchasing a portable door alarm.
- Never leave anything valuable lying around in your room. If you don't have a safe in your room, put it in the hotel safe, or hide it.
- When you are not in your room, keep the TV or radio on, and hang the "Do Not Disturb" sign on the door. If,

possible, have housekeeping clean the room while you are there.

Hotel Fires

A fire can happen at anytime and anywhere. Thousands of people die every year from fires. But when most people stay in a modern hotel, they take for granted that their safety is guaranteed. This isn't always true. Never take this for granted and put your safety into someone else's hands. Many people have done so, and when the time came to take action and escape, they were helpless and many perished needlessly. Many of these people could have avoided death if they had taken the time to plan what to do in the event of a fire.

Planning Ahead

Take the time to do these things every time you check into a hotel:

1. As you are going to your room, take note of where the nearest fire exits are.
2. Once you are in your room, you can also take the time to look at the map that is normally posted on the back of the hotel door. This map will show the fire exit nearest to your room.
3. Walk out of your door toward the nearest fire exit, counting the hotel doors as you do so. In the event you would have to make an escape and it is too smoky to see, you may have to get down on all fours and crawl your way to exit door. By knowing how many doors there are to the fire exit, you will be able to find it by feeling.
4. Once you reach the exit door, take the time to investigate. When you open the door, notice if it locks from the outside. This is so important to know because once you go through the door and let it close, you may be trapped in the stairwell during an emergency. Also, check the door for an alarm.

In Case of a Fire

Remember, the key to survival is to keep your cool and don't panic. Many people have reacted without thinking in this situation and have paid for it with their life. Don't be that person. Have a plan!

If a fire breaks out in your room

- don't try to get to your belongings. Just try to get your door key and get out, making sure you close the door behind you.
- sound the fire alarm, and alert hotel employees.
- knock on nearby room doors to alert the guests.
- don't use the elevator. Use the stairs and get to a safe place.

If you hear the fire alarm or smell smoke

- don't just roll over and ignore it. Call the hotel operator immediately and give your name. Never take any chances when it comes to safety.
- feel the door, before leaving the room. *Never* open a hot door. You will be taking the chance of letting smoke and fire into you room.

If the door is not hot

- call the front desk and ask for the location of the fire.
- peek outside into the hallway to check for smoke. If there is none, grab your key, close your door, and take the stairs to a safe place.

If there is smoke

- place a wet towel, if the smoke is thick, over your nose and mouth and crawl out. The air is better the lower you get.

- as you are leaving, close the door behind you to keep the fire from spreading to your room. You may not be able to see, which is why it is important to know where the exit is ahead of time.
- as you are going down the stairwell, hold onto the rails if there is smoke. If it is too thick, try going up the stairs to a smoke-free hallway and cross the building to an alternate exit. You also may be able to go up to the roof and wait for help.

If the door is hot or there is a fire outside

- stay in the room and be prepared to fight the fire. You must believe you will survive. Just use your head.
- make sure your door is closed tightly, and if there is smoke, wet some towels or clothes and stuff the cracks of the door and the air vents to keep out the smoke.
- and if there is no smoke outside, open the window or sliding door to ventilate the room. Never break the window or door in case the smoke gets too thick outside and you have to close it.
- and if you are on the first or second floor, you should be able to jump safely to the ground, but if you are any higher you may risk injury doing so.
- fill up the bathtub with water and let it overflow. Use a waste basket or an ice bucket to scoop out water to toss on hot doors or walls. Keep the doors and walls wet.
- hang a sheet outside the window to let rescuers know where to find you. Don't try to climb down the sheets.
- and if smoke has entered your room, stand at an open window to breathe fresh air; also place a wet towel over your mouth and nose.

The most important thing you can do in this situation is stay cool and trust your instincts. Your goal is to get out alive, and to listen for the firefighters' instructions.

Take some time now to choose five ways you can make your hotel stay safer:

1.

2.

3.

4.

5.

Chapter Nine

Cruise Ship Safety

I personally love to take vacations on cruises and have taken several over the years. Cruises can be a lot of fun, with the opportunity to visit different places or, if you desire, get away from the rest of the world and just chill out. You go on a vacation to enjoy yourself, but the reality is there are plenty of ways that you can become a victim of crime.

Several years ago on a cruise, my wife and I took an excursion trip to a very popular spot in Jamaica. I had a situation that surprised even me. I broke my own safety rule by pulling out a large amount of cash to make a purchase in a gift shop. Normally I keep my money separate, with a small amount in one pocket and the rest hidden in another pocket. I had forgotten to transfer more money to the small amount, so I took out the large amount without thinking.

After paying for the items, as soon as I walked outside the store I didn't feel right. From experience, I knew something was wrong. I scanned the area and though it was fairly crowded. I saw several Jamaican "cats" coming my way, and they just didn't fit in. Their angry stares and aggressive body language were totally out of place. On closer examination, I noticed one of them had a knife close to his side as he came toward us.

It just so happened I had several knives with me that I had purchased earlier, so I pulled one out and placed it in front of my chest. As soon as they saw it, they backed away. They knew that if I had pulled it out, I was going to use it. I still remember the look on the face of the guy with the knife. As one of his accomplices pulled him away, he was cursing and acting like he wanted to come back.

Interestingly, my wife never knew what was going on, and she was next to me the entire time. Later, after speaking with several of the staff employees, I found out I was set up by the man in the gift shop. He saw the money I was carrying and tipped his boys off. They said I was the first person they knew of to get away from the situation without being robbed. Apparently, this happens all the time, but it's not like the cruise line is going to announce it. That would be bad for business.

If someone is robbed on land, they don't necessarily have time to stick around and help the police look for the criminals. The ship has to stay on schedule. This also isn't considered a large crime, so the employees of the ship aren't always much help. For the criminal, this is great—new people will come in everyday, and once they have robbed someone, chances are the thugs will never see their victims again. I was lucky; because of my awareness skills and reaction to the situation, I was able to prevent myself from becoming a victim. To avoid a cruise disaster, you need to take precautions to ensure that you and your family enjoy yourselves and have a positive experience.

The Safety of the Ships

Cruise ship security did not have to change as much after 9/11 as other aspects of travel, because they have always adhered to strict guidelines. However, they have implemented strengthened security measures in the aftermath.

Here are some things that the cruise lines do to ensure your safety:

- Screening of all passenger carry-on baggage by X-ray.
- Multiple security checkpoints. Expect to pass through three or four before being granted access to your cruise ship.
- Restricted access to any sensitive vessel areas, like the bridge and the engine room.
- Implementing onboard security measures to deter unauthorized entry and illegal activity.
- Requiring all commercial vessels to give ninety-six hours' notice before entering U.S. ports. (Previously, ships only had to give twenty-four hours' notice).
- Maintaining a three hundred-yard security zone around cruise ships and prohibiting private crafts from coming in range. Cruise ships also enlist the assistance of the armed U.S. Coast Guard to escort them in and out of port.
- Expect strict enforcement of required ID and nationality and travel papers. Boarding *will* be denied if you don't have the proper documentation.

These are just a few of the security precautions the cruise industry has taken to ensure passenger safety.

You should take the same precautions as you would for any other trip, such as: protecting your home, bringing everything you need, and getting safely to your destination. The next section outlines a few things you must do to keep your vacation fun and safe.

Safety on the Ships

Over the last few years it has come to the attention of the general public that many crimes such as robbery, grand larceny, rape, and even murder have happened on cruise ships without being reported. Why would the cruise ships not report something this serious? The answer is self-explanatory, but I'm sure no one in the cruise ship business would like to admit it. The fact of the matter is that if they were to report that crimes of this type happen on ships, people would be less inclined to take a vacation on a cruise ship.

To be fair about this particular mode of travel, when you look at the statistics, millions of people cruise every year, and percentage-wise, cruises are relatively safe. Unfortunately, whenever you put people together in an environment like this, it will bring out many types of career criminals who are willing to prey on unsuspecting patrons.

People go on cruises to have fun, and no one wants to be burdened with the day-to-day hassles of being vigilant 24-7 while vacationing. But regardless of where you are, you have to be realistic with yourself and aware of your surroundings in order to keep you and your family safe. When you are on a ship, think of it as a floating hotel. Most of the rules that apply for a hotel can be used in this situation.

Some tips to ensure your safety while cruising are:

- Pay attention to the lifeboat safety drills. Know how to get to them and how to wear life jackets.
- Store all of your valuables, passports, and airline tickets in the room safe. If that doesn't make you feel comfortable, use the ship's safe.
- Keep your door locked at all times.
- Never open your doors to, or invite strangers into, your room.
- Limit the amount of cash you carry when you are on a ship.
- Beware of how much alcohol you are consuming. Don't take a chance of someone taking advantage of you if you are female or as a male, having had one too many, getting into an altercation with someone.

Safety off the Ship

1. Attend all meetings that will be discussing your port of call. Listen carefully for any areas they tell you to avoid.

2. Don't flash your money around or dress like a tourist. Be aware of pickpockets and other people who are out to scam you.
3. In some areas, it would be safer to take the tours that the ships offer than to go off on your own.
4. Make sure you get back to the ship early, because the crew will leave you after a certain time if you are late (make note of any time changes in regards to whatever country you are visiting). This can obviously be a huge inconvenience.

When the cruise is over and you are making your final departure, be sure you have packed everything the night before, but don't pack anything of large value. On most cruises they pick up the luggage the night before, and when you step off the ship, your luggage is waiting for you. Just like the airport, make sure you pick up the right luggage, because someone can easily steal yours. (This is just what happened to me. It was an inconvenience, but I didn't let it ruin my vacation. I reported it, and they reimbursed me for my loss.)

(Review chapter 12: Street Smarts)

Cruises are one of the most enjoyable vacations available, but things can go wrong, especially when you are surrounded by three thousand people from all walks of life and confined in a relatively small area. Follow the advice in this chapter, and you will be much more prepared for your adventure on the high seas.

Take the time to pick three ways you can make your cruise safer:

1.

2.

3.

Chapter Ten

Know the Rules before You Go

Ninety percent of staying safe is awareness. Know the facts before you travel to any destination. It would be foolish to jump on a plane with your family or take a business trip without first knowing something about your destination. If you truly are concerned about staying safe when you travel, you must educate yourself. If it is a place you would typically avoid, do your homework and know what you are dealing with; this way, you have better chance of "coming back alive." In this chapter you will be given many statistics on dangerous places in the world, which will help you gain greater perspective on your travel desires and habits, and what precautions you should be implementing.

Is It Dangerous in America?

The reality is that there are certain places that should be avoided at all costs. Go to any big city or many small towns in America and it is certain that, if you go to the right place at

How To Vacation & Travel Safely

the wrong time, you will be robbed, raped, or even murdered. Is this the way you want to spend your vacation? I don't think so. Most people can travel to any city in the United States and within five minutes find out which areas they should or shouldn't venture to. You will hear the typical warnings about staying clear of the inner-city and low-income area, because someone they knew was robbed there.

This all sounds good in theory; just pinpoint the problems, know where to go, and you will avoid becoming a victim. Well, I wish it were that easy. Granted, the chances of you becoming a victim of crime greatly increase when you venture into certain areas of the big city or drive down a dark country road to play a prank on the local meth dealer. It is not good for your health. It doesn't matter if you know not to go there or not, if you get caught there at the wrong time you will die. Know the rules before you get there. This law of the land can save your life.

Before you start thinking too much about your safety when you travel abroad, let's take a hard look at crime in our own country. Even with all the great advances in technology, and being the richest country in the world, we are also unfortunately one of the most violent countries. Murder, rape, robbery, and aggravated assault happen everywhere every day. Who are the victims of these crimes? If we are not careful, it could be you or me.

The statistics that follow are from the FBI Uniform Crime Reports for the year 2010 by CQPress.com

Note that these numbers could be inaccurate, because not everyone reports a crime in which they are involved.

The Ten Most Dangerous States for Crime

1. Nevada
2. New Mexico
3. Louisiana
4. South Carolina
5. Tennessee

6. Florida
7. Delaware
8. Maryland
9. Arizona
10. Arkansas

The Ten Most Dangerous Cities in the USA

1. St. Louis, MO
2. Camden, NJ
3. Detroit, MI
4. Flint, MI
5. Oakland, CA
6. Richmond, CA
7. Cleveland, OH
8. Compton, CA
9. Gary, IN
10. Birmingham, AL

A great number of tourists travel to these cities each year, and some have fallen victim to crime, including death. Just a few years ago, Florida had the second highest crime rate of all fifty states, and Miami was America's second most dangerous city. Florida had such a huge tourist trade from around the country and abroad that it was open season for criminals. Many tourists were victims of "bump-and-rob" scams, robberies, and sometimes murder. Add the cocaine traffic, which has doubled over the past few years, and you have a huge problem for the state of Florida and their vacation trade.

Fortunately, the state government didn't give up. They had to adjust by creating programs to warn tourists about the problem, and cracking down on criminals. The warnings haven't hurt the vacation trade that much in Florida, which is good, but crime is still a major problem. As of 2003, Florida has not made it back on the "most dangerous state list," but crime still runs rampant in the Sunshine State. Are we supposed to live in fear and not travel? Definitely not, but remember: *vacationers beware!*

Interestingly, Americans tend to be blasé about crime on their own home soil. When you live in a certain city and know the places to avoid, it can be easy to believe the town is safer than it really is. But Europeans citizens have a different perspective that may surprise you.

Places Europeans Consider Most Dangerous

Place	Percentage (%)
1. Florida	42
2. North Africa	9
3. Turkey	7
4. California	7
5. Kenya	7

Is the U.S. dangerous? Yes, it is, but we are used to the crimes that are committed in this country. Although not by choice, we have adapted and continue to live in this country knowing that we have it better than any other country in the world. With that being said, we should take the time to look at where we come from and understand that the same rules may not apply in other parts of the world.

How Safe Is It to Travel Abroad?

So, we know that when you travel abroad there are concerns pertaining to safety. The question is where are the big concerns, and how bad are they in a specific area? You wouldn't want to take the family on vacation to a country where a war is breaking out, would you? Or where there are inordinately high instances of rape or sex trafficking? This is why you have to do your homework. The good news is there are ways to find out what kinds of violence are happening in other countries.

There is information available on every type of crime committed in every country around the world. Here's an uncomfortable truth: the info given to us is not always accurate. According to Ben Best at "Death by Murder" at www.geocities.com, international murder rates for cities are difficult to obtain outside of the developed world. Several of these countries listed have some of the highest murder rates in the world, but there are no reliable statistics, and Interpol refuses to make its statistics public. *Why?* Because if the real numbers were revealed, it would cause grave concern about traveling in these particular areas.

When it comes to making a list of the most dangerous countries from around the world, we have to break it down with two lists. Forbes.com created its most dangerous list with countries that have a history of war, conflict, terrorism, and violence. If you travel to any of these countries, unless you are completely out of the loop, you know that you are walking into trouble, and there is a good chance you may not be coming back.

Ten Most Dangerous Countries in the World for 2010, According to Forbes.com

1. Somalia
2. Afghanistan
3. Iraq
4. Democratic Republic of Congo
5. Pakistan
6. Gaza, Palestinian Territories
7. Sri Lanka
8. Yemen
9. Sudan
10. Zimbabwe

This next list consists of the countries that are traveled to for vacation and business, even though there is a history of crime that includes drugs, kidnapping, robberies, and murder. Travelers beware.

Top Ten Most Dangerous Countries for Tourists

1. Colombia
2. South Africa
3. Jamaica

4. Venezuela
5. Russia
6. Mexico
7. Brazil
8. Philippines
9. Haiti
10. Nigeria

Like certain countries there are cities around the world that are popular destinations for vacationers and those who like to travel. The rules of personal safety should be followed even more so when traveling to these foreign cities. This list consists of the cities that overwhelmingly showed up on the lists of the most dangerous cities in 2010.

Most Dangerous Cities in the World (2010)

- Caracas, Venezuela
- Ciudad Juarez, Mexico
- Detroit, USA
- Mogadishu, Somalia
- Cape Town, South Africa
- Bogotá, Columbia
- Rio de Janeiro, Brazil
- Grozny, Chechnya, Russia
- Baghdad, Iraq
- New Orleans, USA
- Guatemala City, Guatemala
- Bangkok, Thailand

It has been reported that in Colombia, 75 percent of murders were a result of street crime and common criminals, while the remaining 25 percent were attributed to guerrilla activity and narcotic-terrorists. Cocaine is Colombia's number one export. This makes the country a dangerous place to live and an even worst place to visit. Another crime that is running rampant against tourists is robbery. It will continue to be a growing problem as long as vacationers and travelers make it easy for thieves. *The Daily Telegraph* (3/23/03) listed the top ten cities from around the world where you have a greater chance of getting robbed:

- Kingston, Jamaica
- Rio de Janeiro, South America
- Cape Town, South Africa
- Mexico City, Mexico
- St. Petersburg, Russia
- Buenos Aires, Argentina
- Bangkok, Thailand
- Washington, DC
- Rome, Italy
- Athens, Greece

Each of these cities is an extremely popular vacation spot. When the average person plans for his or her vacation, personal safety or avoiding becoming a victim of crime is not a top priority until it actually happens. The *number one rule* is to always be aware of what is going on around you and stay alert. The second rule is to never consume drugs or alcohol while out in public. Besides the obvious problems of taking drugs, if you get caught in a foreign country with them, you could very well spend the rest of your life in that country's jail with no way of getting out.

Drinking alcohol can impair your decision-making process and make you an easy target for a criminal. Only drink around your family or close friends. Be leery of strangers or anyone who wants to suddenly be your best friend. The golden rule of travel is not to trust anyone. That way the chances of enjoying yourself and having a safe vacation are on your side; you can make sure that the odds remain in your favor by keeping a "safety first" attitude.

Real Life: "Vacation from Hell"

One real-life story that will hopefully give you insight into exactly what vacationers are up against is the always celebrated, but sometimes loathed "paid excursion" off the resort premises.

How To Vacation & Travel Safely

You know the routine. The days on the beach often grow tiring and thrill seekers are looking for a change from the hotel room. So what do they do? They dish out a couple extra hundred dollars for a safari excursion, deep-sea fishing, shopping tour or other adventure away from the resort. Nine times out of ten these trips are safe and a wonderful addition to your vacation, but there are unscrupulous people out there who seek to earn extra money by unethical means.

Case in point: a couple went on the aforementioned safari excursion which initially was advertised at one particular set price. In this instance, the tour guides demanded more cash from the guests, threatening to leave them in the middle of the jungle if they did not get it. The couple was forced to cough up the extra money in exchange for their wellbeing. The lesson here is to make sure that all off-resort excursions are hosted by legitimate companies, preferably recommended by the hotel or travel company with whom you booked the trip. The last thing you want is to be stranded in the middle of a rain forest, wearing only your swimming suit and your bug spray.

Chapter Eleven

Safely Traveling Overseas

One of life's greatest experiences is to be able to travel abroad. I didn't really learn about life until I went to other countries and met people of different nationalities and cultures. I wouldn't trade anything for the experiences I've had while traveling. One thing I learned very quickly, however, is that you cannot go to other countries and do the same things you do in the good old U.S.A. When traveling internationally, there are certain rules you and your family must abide by in order to insure everyone will have fun and, most importantly, stay safe.

Unfortunately, in some parts of the world Americans are not well liked; we are accepted because of the money we bring to the country's economy. But that doesn't stop thousands of tourists from becoming victims of crime. Another problem that occurs more often than you'd suspect is the kidnapping for ransom of American business people from all over the world. This problem is so common that there is insurance for this type of crime. It happens so often that most people who travel overseas for business know there is a high probability they can be a victim of this. With that being said, no one should have to live in fear, or base their right to travel and have fun on a smaller percentage of crimes that happen every year.

Planning for Overseas Travel

We live in an imperfect world. Besides being concerned about you and your family's safety while you are traveling, there are many other things you should take stock of. What would you do if you or one of your family members got sick while you were vacationing overseas? Even worse, what if you or one of your family members suddenly died? How would you handle being on vacation on a tropical island if it were hit by a hurricane or tsunami? What if someone snatches your purse or wallet? Inside could be your passport, visa, credit cards, and cash. These items could be stolen without any way to replace them.

Understand this: you, and *only* you, are responsible for your safety. Yes, there are police in just about every country in the world, but if you get into trouble and are in need of assistance, the police are not always willing to come to the aid of an American. If you do get their assistance, and you need help from the U.S. or help going back home, it may not be that easy. So the best way to deal with the unexpected is to prepare ahead of time. Before you leave on any trip, educate yourself on what you need to know, what you need to do and when, and what you can and cannot take on your trip abroad. Traveling abroad doesn't have to be a negative experience; you just have to know where to go, where not to go, and the rules before you get there.

Putting Affairs in Order

- If you do not already have them, apply for a passport and visa at least four months before you leave.
- Put all important papers (insurance, will, house deeds) in a safe place (safe deposit box at bank or in a safe at home) or in the hands of a trusted family member or attorney.

Remember, if you are deceased and no one knows where you stashed anything, chances are they never will which will only complicate matters regarding your estate.
- Get the phone number to the American embassy in the country in which you will be staying.
- Check travel advisories to determine if there is a warning in the country you are traveling to. Don't walk into a bad situation if you don't have to.
- If you are planning to stay for an extended duration, you must obtain an international driving permit.
- Make sure all your immunizations are up to date and consider having a tetanus shot. Certain third world counties still have strains of diseases that are no longer much of a threat in America.
- Consider asking your doctor for a prescription of antibiotics.

What to Learn before You Go

In the computer age, there are various ways to obtain information about what is happening around the world. According to the Department of State Publication and Bureau of Consular Affairs, the Consular Information Sheets provide information about crime and security conditions, political disturbances, and areas of instability. They also provide addresses and emergency telephone numbers for U.S. embassies and consulates. The sheets do not give advice. Instead, they describe conditions, so travelers can make informed decisions about their trip. In some dangerous situations, The Department of State will issue a "travel warning" to Americans against traveling to a particular area.

The most convenient source of information about traveling and consulate services is the Consular Affairs home page. The Web site is http://travel.state.gov. The Overseas Citizens Services (888-407-4747) will answer general questions on safety and security overseas.

It is always very important that travelers know about the local laws and customs of the country they are going to. You will be subject to their laws. In order to become educated in these matters, information may be obtained through reliable sources such as travel agents, the library, embassies, consulates, or tourist bureaus of the country you will visit.

Here are some tips to make your trip abroad a safe one:

1. Leave a copy of your itinerary with family members or friends in case of an emergency.
2. Make two photocopies of everything of importance that you will carry, i.e., passports, airline tickets, credit cards, and driver's license. Leave one photocopy of these items with a trusted family member or friend, and pack the other copies separate from your valuables that you carry on your trip.
3. Research the political situation of that area including any instability or related crimes.
4. Learn the laws and customs of your destination country as you will be subject to their rules.
5. Consider purchasing a telephone calling card should your cell phone not work in certain areas. If you get one, verify that it can be used from your overseas location.
6. Dress in a low-key manner. Do not flaunt the fact that you are an American. Less is best.
7. Avoid being robbed. Leave any valuable jewelry or watches at home, especially when you travel alone. If you must take them, hide them in different pieces of luggage. Lock your cash, credit cards, and passport in the hotel safe when you get there.
8. Have enough money in your purse or pocket to give to a robber in the unfortunate event that you are robbed. If you don't have anything, he may become violent. If you have not been trained in self-defense, it is best to know when to pick your battles.
9. If you wear glasses or contacts, pack an extra pair in your carry-on luggage.
10. To avoid problems when passing through customs, keep medicines in their original containers in your carry-on luggage.

11. Make sure your luggage tags contain your name, phone number, and street address. The information should be concealed from casual observation.

Traveling Day

Going through Airport Security and Customs

In chapter six we covered the basics of how to make trips to the airport as smooth as possible. There are additional steps you can take to move quickly through the security process. The following should help make your airport experience less of a headache.

- You should always plan ahead and pack smart for your trip. Don't over pack. If a bag weighs over fifty pounds, you will be asked to take things out and put them in a different bag or be forced to pay a fee. If the weather permits, you should pack a light jacket or coat.
- Don't pack anything that can be considered a weapon.
- Dress comfortably, keeping in mind that certain clothing and accessories can set off the metal detector and slow you down. Avoid wearing belts with metal buckles, shoes with steel tips or heels, any type of jewelry including body piercing, or anything else with metal on it.
- Be aware of items in your pockets that can set off the alarm. Loose change, keys, and cell phones are a few of the things that you may forget until it is too late. The easiest thing you can do would be to pack all items that may set off the metal detector in your carry-on baggage, until you clear security.
- Passengers are limited to one carry-on and one personal item. Always place ID tags on all of your baggage.
- Arrive early, with the proper documents.
- Luggage should be checked curbside or at the ticket counter. Items of value should remain with you in your carry-on, so they won't be stolen.

- Don't be surprised if you are randomly selected for additional screening at the departure gate.
- People with special needs such as disabilities, medical concerns, or those traveling with children should get to the airport early.

Avoiding Legal Difficulties

One of the biggest misconceptions Americans have when they are abroad is that they are under the protection of the American Constitution. *This is not true.* When you are in a foreign country, you are subject to the laws of that country. Be aware of what is considered criminal in the country where you are traveling. Consular information sheets include information on unusual patterns or arrests.

Some of the offenses for which U.S. citizens have been arrested abroad include the following:

1. *Drug violations.* Drug possession and use is the single largest reason U.S. citizens are arrested abroad. The laws vary according to the country you are in. Check with the local authorities or the nearest U.S. embassy or consulate for details.
2. *Firearm possession.* The illegal possession of firearms in most countries comes with a stiff penalty, sometimes up to thirty years in prison. Registered firearms in the United States cannot be transported into another country without first obtaining a permit. Obtaining a permit is not worth the hassle. It is best to not even try to deal with the problems that go along with carrying a firearm abroad.
3. *Photography.* In many counties you can be detained or harassed for taking pictures of police and military installations, government buildings, border areas and transportation facilities. If you are in doubt, ask permission before taking pictures.
4. *Purchasing antiques.* Americans have been incarcerated for buying and/or trying to secretly ship certain antiques

and paintings out of different countries. In countries where antiques are important they are considered national treasures. If your purchases are reproductions, then document them as such, and if they are authentic, secure the necessary export permits.

The Truth about Our Safety Abroad: Terrorism

Fact: With political unrest and terrorism arising all over the globe, it is imperative to keep an eye on any problems that can erupt in a country where you will be visiting for business or pleasure. The last thing you want to do is land right in the middle of turmoil. Unfortunately, acts of terrorism usually occur unexpectedly, making them almost impossible for the average citizen to anticipate. That doesn't mean you should stay at home fearful of traveling and having a good time, but a rational person has to make smart choices when they are planning to take themselves and their family on a trip.

It should be common knowledge by now that people should avoid traveling to unsafe areas with a record of terrorism or kidnapping. Most terrorist attacks are the result of long and careful planning. They are looking for easily accessible targets that follow predictable patterns. The chances of a tourist becoming a victim of such an attack are slim, but not impossible. Most terrorist groups are seeking publicity for their political causes.

How to Avoid Becoming a Target of Opportunity

- Schedule direct flights, if possible, and avoid stops in high risk airports or areas. Consider other options of travel when not crossing water, such as trains.
- One should be aware of what is discussed with strangers or what others may overhear.
- Try to minimize time spent in public areas of the airport, which are less protected. Move quickly from the check-in counter to the secured areas. On arrival, leave the airport as soon as possible.

How To Vacation & Travel Safely

- When possible, avoid luggage tags, dress, and behavior that may identify you as an American.
- Keep an eye out for suspicious abandoned packages or briefcases. Repeat them to airport security or other authorities and leave the area promptly.

Traveling in High Risk Areas

If you must travel in an area where there has been a history of terrorist attacks or kidnapping, take the following steps:

1. Discuss with your family what they would do in the event of an emergency. Make sure your affairs are in order before leaving home.
2. Let someone else know what your travel plans are. Keep them informed if you change your plans.
3. Register with the U.S. embassy or consulate upon arrival.
4. Remain friendly but cautious about discussing personal matters, such as your itinerary or programs, with strangers or people you have just met.
5. Leave no personal or business papers in your hotel room.
6. Always be certain of a visitor's identity before opening your hotel door. Don't meet strangers at unknown or remote locations.
7. Refuse unexpected packages.
8. Watch for people following you or loiters observing your schedule.
9. Avoid predictable times, routes, and travel, and report any suspicious activity to local police and the nearest U.S. embassy or consulate.
10. Keep a mental note of safe havens, such as police stations, hotels, and hospitals.
11. Select your own taxicab at random. Don't take a vehicle that is not clearly identified as a taxi. Compare the face of the driver with the one posted on his or her license.

12. Formulate a plan of action for what you will do if a bomb explodes or there is gunfire nearby.
13. Make sure your rental vehicle is in good operating condition, in case you need to resort to high speed or evasive driving.
14. Check for loose wires or other suspicious activity around your rental car.
15. Drive with your car widows up in crowded streets. Bombs can be thrown through open windows.
16. If in a situation where someone is shooting, drop to the floor or get down as far as you can, or behind something that is solid. Don't move until you are sure the danger has passed.

(Review chapter Six for hijacking/hostage situations)

Assistance Abroad

If you need assistance while abroad, the consulate in the U.S. embassy will do the following:

1. Assist in getting a new passport if yours is lost or stolen.
2. Provide information on the security situation in a country.
3. Provide a list of local physicians and medical facilities if you become ill or injured. If the illness or injury is serious, consulate officers can help you attain medical assistance, and inform your family or friends back home.
4. Help you get in touch with your family, friends, bank or employer if your money is depleted and inform them how to wire funds to you.
5. Provide a list of local attorneys who speak English if legal difficulties arise, who may have experience in representing U.S. citizens. Consulate officers cannot serve as attorneys, give legal advice, or get you out of jail.
6. If arrested, consulate officials will visit and advise you of your rights under the local laws and ensure fair and humane treatment under the local laws. A consulate

officer will also contact your family and friends, if you desire. (*via http://travel.state.gov*)

If you are detained in another country, under international law and international treaties, you have the right to speak with a U.S. consul.

Dealing with Overseas Airports

Upon reaching your destination, keep a low profile as you go through the airport to pick up your luggage. Verify your luggage to make sure it is yours. Once you have it, don't ever leave it or your carry-on baggage. Never carry anyone else's bags, and stay away from baggage that has been left unattended.

This may sound a little paranoid, but be aware of your surroundings and exits and places of safety in the event something happens where you will have to exit immediately or take cover.

Safety While Driving Abroad

When renting a car, do your best to get a vehicle that is commonly driven in that area and, where possible, one that doesn't have any markings to show that it is a rental car. Make sure the car runs well and has an air conditioner, along with power locks and power windows.

Again, always drive with your window closed, which will hinder thieves from trying to snatch a purse or valuables through an open window, or from committing a carjacking against you. Carjackers and thieves love to scope out their victims at popular tourist places like parking lots, gas stations, and even city traffic. Unfortunately, you can't trust anyone. Remember the following tips:

- Know where you are going ahead of time. Most people will be nice and try to help you, but if the wrong person is asked for directions, they can send you to the wrong place and set you up for a robbery.

- As you are driving keep the doors locked and wear your seat belts at all times.
- Avoid night driving when possible.
- Don't leave valuables in your car. If you must, then keep them out of sight or in the trunk.
- If possible, don't park your car on the street. Try to park in a garage or another secure place.
- Never pick up hitchhikers.
- Never get out of the car if something looks suspicious. Trust your instincts and drive away.

(For additional car safety tips, review chapter Four: Car Safety on the Road)

Safety on Public Transportation

Unfortunately, when traveling abroad to certain places, there will be criminals who feel their job is to seek and find unsuspecting tourists just like you, and steal or rob from you any way they can. The average tourist makes it easy for criminals by going to the same places tourists usually frequent. Tourists get robbed and beaten all over the world while on vacation, but most of them never report it because they know the criminals will never be found.

Tourists like to congregate in the same places. One popular item criminals steal besides money is the passport. Stolen passports can be sold for a thousand dollars each on the black market and are always in high demand. The most common problem is pickpocketing, followed by car vandalism.

One of the most popular places for crime, especially pickpocketing, is any mode of public transportation. Because the crowds can be large, this is the ideal time for pickpockets to "do their thing." Another area for potential crime would be public restrooms.

Once you are on the subway, bus or train, follow the rules that apply to transportation safety. Refer to the chapters listed below:

Chapter Five: Bus and Train Safety
Chapter Seven: Safely Getting to Your Destination

To prevent becoming a victim, the key is to stay alert and be on guard. Trust no one!

Take some time now to list five ways to travel safely when abroad:

1.

2.

3.

4.

5.

Chapter Twelve

Business Travel Safety

When the average American vacations abroad, the chances of being kidnapped or killed due to terrorism are slim, but if one is an executive and traveling for business, different rules apply. No longer considered an "ordinary American," extra security precautions should be taken. Understand that danger is a possibility every time an American executive travels to another country. *But why?*

Let's go back briefly to the earlier discussion about how Americans are perceived in other countries. In most places we are tolerated as tourists because we spend a lot of money, which will help their economy grow and create new jobs for their people. Robbers and muggers are also very happy when tourists visit their country. Remember my advice: *don't look or act like a tourist.* In most places you visit, as long as you don't come across as overly patriotic, flying the American flag or doing anything that can be misconstrued as being disrespectful of that country, you should be safe.

The rules change when dealing with a business executive from the United States. Not only are we disliked by many foreigners because of the propaganda that is spread about Americans, but some hate the fact that, if they want their country and economy to stay strong and survive, they must do business with Americans. Many business people have no idea how vulnerable they are when they travel. They don't even worry about their security until they are confronted by a dangerous crime being committed against them or their loved ones. This is too little, too late. The one thing we do know is that most terrorists kidnap business people for money or to gain publicity for their cause. The question is: "Could I ever be chosen as a victim of kidnapping?" If so, how can you effectively protect yourself against this type of crime?

The first thing to determine is if you fit into what is called the "terrorist profile." First, terrorists may select you as a target if you appear to be wealthy. One of the most common denominators of all terrorist groups is that they need money to operate. You don't always have to be wealthy yourself, but if you work for a large American company and are considered an important executive, your employer will have kidnapping insurance for you, and will be able to pay a hefty ransom for your safe return.

How can you prevent a potential terrorist from choosing to kidnap you because of your station? The only real way is not to have any wealth. I don't think anyone who has worked hard to be successful would be willing to lower their lifestyle and not enjoy the fruits of their labor because there is a chance (a small chance) that someone is out to get them. The threat is real, but I'd bet any successful businessperson will take the chance and enjoy his or her huge house, expensive car, and private school for the kids and not feel guilty about their success. Why? Because this person earned them.

Second, do you represent something or someone important? Terrorists need publicity, and they need to keep their causes in the public eye. Kidnapping someone who is not important will not accomplish this. So if you represent a huge American company with a worldwide image, you will most likely become a target.

If you are a top-level executive in a well-known corporation, it will be pretty hard to keep low-key and behind the scenes. The higher up the ladder you go, the more important you will become to the company you are employed by, and the more your name will float around important circles. Unfortunately, terrorists keep up with this type of information.

Third, how accessible are you? Terrorists, like everyone else, seek the path of least resistance. They will watch you and study your habits before they make the decision to kidnap. If they feel an executive will be easy to kidnap and is accessible, most likely that person will be their next target. As a potential victim of a kidnapping, if your company does not already have insurance or a plan for your safety, you must take matters into your own hands. There are many different aspects of safety when it comes to a business executive. I could write a whole book on this subject alone, but for the sake of this book, I will stick to the subject of travel safety for the executive.

Executives are very busy people. They assume, "If it isn't broke, don't fix it." The company is asking, "Why should we spend money on the security of our executives? No one is going to bother them." This kind of shortsightedness can put the whole company in jeopardy. Any high profile person of wealth—in business, entertainment, or otherwise—must be careful where they go and what they do. Because of my self-defense and bodyguard training, I teach all of my clients to think like a bodyguard. Don't wait until someone tragic like a kidnapping, or worse, an assassination, occurs.

Take an honest assessment of your situation and ask yourself, *"As an executive, do I need to take my safety seriously?"* The greatest single factor in reducing your risk to terrorism is to take active security precautions. Only *you* are responsible for your safety.

Threat Assessment

Making a threat assessment of your situation and a plan on how to keep safe while you travel is crucial. As a businessperson, what threats should you be concerned with?

Assassination. The most likely target of this crime is political leaders. This is not to say that the assassination of a businessperson could not happen. If a businessman or woman associates with a political leader, or the company they work for is involved in a politically controversial practice, this could also put him or her in danger of being assassinated.

Kidnapping. The average person does not have to worry about kidnapping; however, business executives, celebrities, and other people of wealth are not average people. Kidnapping runs rampant in several overseas countries, and money is generally the reason executives are targeted. Your company needs to have kidnapping insurance in place for you.

Street Violence. Robberies, carjacking, and even murder can happen for many reasons, but the one thing that can make an executive stand out could be his or her appearance. If you dress like most businesspeople while in another country doing business—i.e., Rolex watches, etc.—you take the chance of putting yourself in harm's way and becoming a victim of crime, especially if you are alone.

Embarrassment. Being made to look badly can be something as simple as falling down the steps as you are walking off the stage after a motivational speech, to something as serious as having pictures taken of you while you are entertaining a group of women at a strip club. Think and see the big picture before you go out and do something that may come back to haunt you.

There are many other situations you can put on this list, but they are small in comparison to the situations listed above. Any one of these could escalate into a very bad scene, which is why you must take the steps to plan your protection.

Where Are the Most Dangerous Places for Executives to Travel?

According to Robert Young Pelton's book *The World's Most Dangerous Places,* businesspeople are the greatest targets for terrorists and thugs alike. They make excellent kidnapping victims as well as willing dispensers of cash for bribes (p. 69).

The most dangerous places for business travel are:

- Algeria
- Angola
- Colombia
- Mexico
- Nigeria
- Pakistan
- The Philippines
- Russia

Although business travel is the most dangerous type of excursion, it has not slowed down the thousands of businessmen and women who venture into war torn or drug-infested countries to earn the almighty dollar. Billions of dollars are made every year in overseas business, both legally and illegally. With so much money to be made, you will always find someone who is willing to take a chance to venture into a country that is considered dangerous. Terrorists know that huge corporations doing business in their country can compensate them handsomely, and with so much money at stake, the bigwigs at the helm of huge conglomerates consider a kidnapping or an occasional murder the price of doing business.

If you must travel to an unsafe location and are sane enough to be worried, first find out as much about the area you are traveling to as possible. Large corporations have security departments that will provide a briefing on any country. Second, learn about the culture and customs as well as the local laws of the country you are visiting. The worst thing to happen would be to get into trouble for something that you considered minor, and then end up spending the next thirty years of your life in a third world prison.

If you don't have a personal bodyguard, hire one. If you cannot or there is not enough time to do so, do the next best thing and start thinking like one.

Preparing to Travel to Your Destination

To most people, international travel seems like a huge perk of a job. Yes, there is a status to traveling around the world and staying in luxurious and expensive hotels, working and making important decisions for huge corporations, but it is still work and can pose risks. Along with the stress and demands of the job, be aware of the safety concerns in foreign countries:

- Make an honest threat assessment of your proposed destination.
- Make your reservation strategically. If flying commercially, select a well-known airline and try to secure a nonstop flight. Preferably, have the host company make your flight, hotel, and car reservations, choose the safest places to stay, and do so discreetly. Stay low-key and do not advertise to potential enemies that are traveling to the area.
- Pack lightly, taking only what is necessary.
- Mentally rehearse each aspect of your trip from a security perspective. Have a plan from the time you arrive at the airport to go to your destination, to the time you leave the country and return to the States.
- While traveling, keep in communication with your company or someone you trust in the event you should run into any difficultly while traveling.
- Again, be as low-key and unassuming as possible.

Preparation Upon Arriving at Terminal

Spend minimal time when going to the airport. If you are going to check your luggage curbside, watch to make sure that it actually is put on the conveyer and is going to be loaded.

Most airlines have corporate club memberships for executives who travel internationally. The executives may use the lounge, which is located in a restricted area; however, being in a restricted area does not guarantee safety. In the event that an executive does not have a restricted area in which to stay while waiting for a flight, he or she must take the precautions outlined in chapter Six to ensure his or her safety.

Some tips for staying safe in an airport terminal are:

- While waiting, keep your back to the wall so you can view what is going on around you.
- Keep your guard up and be leery of people who seem out of place or who want to start unnecessary conversations.
- Avoid sitting by windows. If gunshots are fired or bombs have exploded, this will reduce the possibility of flying glass hitting you.
- In the event you have to go to the restroom, do so with caution. This could be a perfect place to commit several types of crimes, including robbery or a terrorist attack. Men should avoid stalls when possible and try to pick a urinal situated to allow you to see who has entered the restroom after you.
- In the event an explosion does occur or you hear gunshots, try to position yourself behind a pillar or something that can shield you. If there is nothing available, drop to the ground and cover your head for protection with your briefcase or whatever else is available.

Your Safety During the Flight

Currently airport security is at an all-time high, making it more difficult to hijack planes. The average businessperson doesn't seem worried about flying first class, and surely the prestige and amenities outweigh the worry of someone taking over the plane.

But top-level executives are encouraged to fly coach on commercial flights. In the event there is a hijacking, if you are flying first class, the terrorists will assume that you are someone of importance. The key hijacker will position himself in the first class section near the cockpit. If the plane is taken by force, the cockpit/first class area will be under fire from both sides.

The most preferable section would be in the rear of the aircraft as close to the main door as possible. Always try to sit in a center or window seat, because if a hostage selection takes place in the coach section, the aisle seats have much better chance of being chosen by a nervous hijacker. Also, if a firefight takes place, the angle of fire will be up and down the aisle, with the aisle seat in the line of fire. Window and center seats on the other hand, give substantial protection.

Company or Private Aircraft

In today's business world, more and more executives are getting around in a private jet. The convenience of not having to fight the crowd to go through the airport, and the prestige that goes along with having a private plane at your disposal, can make you look and feel very successful.

Here are some tips for traveling via provided aircraft:

- Keep the departure times and dates on a need-to-know basis.
- Don't give the pilots or the flight company a list of the passenger names until necessary.
- If you use a private or company-owned plane, arrange for a private, security-patrolled area in which to park.
- Upon reaching your destination, ensure that the plane is in a safe and well-lit area.
- Cabin doors should remain locked until boarding time for crew and passengers.
- Require that the pilot examine all interior and cargo bins in the plane prior to all departures.
- When possible, remove all company insignias and logos from the aircraft.
- Have your security personnel sweep the plane before each departure.
- All baggage taken aboard must be identified.
- Any visitors to the operation/maintenance areas must be escorted by security and/or authorized company personnel.
- Any maintenance or cabin service personnel who board the aircraft should be accompanied by a crewmember.

- If the safety of a plane has been compromised in any way, it must be evacuated and thoroughly searched by security personnel.

Common sense training along with awareness and personal responsibility are the common denominators for corporations to consider in their strategies for preparedness regarding executive safety. It is far better to have planned a security program in advance.

The Need for an Advance Person

Once an executive gets to his or her destination, it would be to their advantage to work with a person who lives in the country and is employed by the host company. Anytime you are visiting as a high-level executive, you need people who know the country and environment, and who have access to the resources to keep you safe. An advance person is there to keep you on schedule and out of trouble—from making sure you are picked up from the airport to checking in ahead of time, getting you to the hotel, getting you to scheduled meetings, and also to dinner with other business people.

Here is an abridged list of things an advance person should excel at. If you don't have a bodyguard, you can apply these same tactics yourself.

- Urban camouflage (the ability to blend, rather than attract attention).
- Selecting the routes and times of your travel.
- Planning an itinerary for safe travel.
- Selecting hotels for your stay.
- Establishing a security team.
- Protection while walking.
- Protection in the vehicle or airplane.
- Taking control of the environment in general to limit access.

- Reducing the client's exposure to possible danger by getting him or her from point A to point B along the safest routes.
- Establishing a safe area atmosphere for the client, wherever they may go.
- Preserving the client's valuable time by eliminating unnecessary waiting or time wasting. The goal of the advance person is to keep his or her client moving.

An advance person can be worth their weight in gold. By taking care of all the work before your arrival, they give you peace of mind and allow you to take care of business at hand. Keep in mind, this person may work for your company or the host company, or he or she could be a bodyguard hired to protect you during your stay.

Tips for staying safe during business travel:

- Don't get too friendly with the locals. You can inadvertently inform them of your vacation plans, where you are staying and even your business plans. This could be information they can sell for big money. Never discuss your plans, accommodations, finances, or politics with strangers.
- Avoid eating at restaurants frequented by tourists. Don't make reservations in your name, and do not eat outside.
- Don't reveal your home address or phone number or show your wallet when meeting people. Use a P.O. Box or your business address.
- Leave all expensive jewelry at home.
- When in your hotel room, remember where the exit doors are in case of an emergency, and keep you door locked at all times.
- Vary your schedule and change your routes when you travel. Kidnappers need prior warning or tip-offs to do their dirty work.
- Don't accept a drink unless you watch it being poured.

How to Know If You Are a Target

A business executive knows his or her value to the company and how much it can hurt and disrupt the company if something were to happen. This means that a terrorist or kidnapper could acquire the same information. One of the most popular ways they get information about you is to have a *tail* follow you to determine your schedule, where you are going, and what will be the best place and time to get to you. A terrorist's best defense is their anonymity. When this protection is removed, they become naked and extremely vulnerable. This is why you should have a personal security program that is well-planned and followed exactly. Your goal: if and when terrorists come after you, it will be too difficult to do so, and not worth the effort.

Before they can come after you, they must find out your habits through *surveillance*. Here are some ways they may do this:

- Most surveillance efforts begin where you are staying and continue to your final destination.
- It will cover your daily routine.
- It will take place with more than one vehicle to maintain covert status.
- The kidnappers/terrorists will surveil with regularity and with the same team.
- Most of the best surveillance teams are linked to those employed by governments, elite law enforcement, and a select group of terrorist organizations.

Tactics of Professional Surveillance While in a Vehicle

Parallel surveillance is conducted by two or more vehicles. One vehicle tails the victim at a reasonable distance, while the other driver or drivers follow on parallel streets ready to take up close quarter surveillance should the victim turn. This method will not work in areas where there are no parallel roads.

Leap Frog surveillance: One surveillant tails the victim closely while his partner stays well ahead of both vehicles. The great advantage to this is that the tailing vehicle can fall far behind while the lead vehicle slows down and establishes visual contact. Also, the tailing and lead vehicle can exchange positions to avoid detection.

Electronic tracking: A tracker is placed on the underside of the victim's car where it will be harder to see. There are many types of trackers, and they are usually attached to the vehicle with powerful magnets. There are two ways to determine if you are a victim of this device. The first would be to make a complete visual inspection of the underside of the vehicle. The second is to use a sophisticated electronic device that can detect radio transmissions.

It is easiest to detect a single surveillant. Professionals, whether governmental or private, rarely conduct surveillance using a single person, because there is a greater risk of being caught. A lone surveillant must stay close enough to keep you in sight, yet far enough away to avoid detection. This is not an easy feat.

But even the most experienced surveillance teams can make mistakes or perform actions that can make them detectable by their target, if he or she knows what to look for. In order to successfully detect surveillance, awareness skills must be used and eyes kept open.

Here are a few tips on how to detect a surveillance team:

- Trust your eyes, and believe what you are seeing. If you see a particular vehicle or person more than once in a certain amount of time, this may not be a coincidence. If the person or vehicle is following you or you see them near the hotel where you are staying this can possibly mean someone is doing surveillance on you.
- Most surveillance will use more than one vehicle, so don't become fixated on just one vehicle. Any intelligent group will be wise enough to switch vehicles and personnel to throw off their target.
- If you suspect you are being followed, make notes as to the description of both people and vehicles, and the times and places they are seen.

- Whatever you do, don't let the people shadowing you know that they have been detected. You will lose the *edge* you have on them. You should report this to your security staff or the local U.S. embassy.
- If you are dealing with a legitimate surveillance, avoid a personal confrontation if at all possible. Do not take a situation like this lightly, especially if you are visiting a country that has a known terrorist environment.

Vehicle Safety and Security

The most vulnerable time for most executives is when they are going to and from their various destinations while traveling abroad. There are several weak links of which you should be aware.

- Where you are staying.
- Where you are working.
- Where you are visiting (going out to dinner, going to bars and social visits).
- Your routes to and from the aforementioned places.

Vehicle safety should be one of the most vital parts of your personal safety program. Every morning when you get into your car, you are facing the most dangerous part of the day in terms of dealing with kidnappers and terrorists. Terrorists love this part of your daily routine because they can easily select the location and conditions in which to make their move on you. Despite all of your precautions, it will be during this time you are the most vulnerable.

There are two areas of vehicle and driving safety that need to be examined. The first and most important one is prevention. Prevention is avoiding selection as a target of kidnapping. The second area of vehicle safety is the way you react to being attacked. When we say react, this means recognizing the fact that you are being attacked, and knowing how to drive away from the attack.

Prevention

Since this book is based on the fact that you are responsible for your own safety and well-being, prevention is the easiest way to maintain your vehicle safety. If you have done a good job of protecting yourself at your hotel, and in whichever corporate setting you are working, the terrorist will have to find out how secure you are in your vehicle. The way they get this information is, as recently discussed, through surveillance of their target. If they feel your security is good, they will seek someone else out as a target to kidnap.

How to avoid being a victim while behind the wheel:

- A large part of your vehicle safety program is the ability to detect surveillance. Detecting surveillance is the best method you have to avoid becoming a target.
- Stay away from areas of a city that are considered dangerous. In many third world cities, this is almost impossible. You must use caution when driving through areas you know to be dangerous.
- Become familiar with all the possible routes you will be using throughout the day. Become unpredictable when traveling in your vehicle. You need to know shortcuts in the event a problem arises.
- Wear your seat belt, and adjust seat, mirrors, and steering wheel for individual use.
- Keep moving. A moving target is harder to hit than a stationary one.
- Avoid driving too closely behind other vehicles, and be aware of activities and road conditions two or three blocks ahead. If there is a situation that requires you to stop, don't drive up to the incident. Hold back and see what develops or take an alternate route.
- Try to stay on busy, well-traveled roads. Avoid isolated back roads.
- Drive an air-conditioned vehicle so that you can keep the windows up. This will prevent someone from throwing

something into the vehicle, or sticking a gun or hand inside.
- Always keep doors locked while traveling.
- Keep a charged cell phone, so you can stay in contact with your place of destination.
- Avoid suspicious roadblocks. This could be a setup.
- When possible, drive a couple of different vehicles during your trip to avoid visual familiarity.
- Consider taking a defensive driving course, if you will be driving abroad with any regularity.

The best line of defense for an executive is unpredictability. The location of the potential target must be difficult to pinpoint; unfortunately, most executives are not willing to accept this element of unpredictability, because it is too much of a change in their lifestyle.

Type of Vehicle

Whichever type of vehicle you drive must blend in with the existing cars in that particular country. Don't rent a Bentley. Besides being easy to locate, it could tempt a carjacker or robber to make you their next victim. If you can't get a bulletproof armored vehicle, the next best thing is to get a vehicle that will best serve your needs when it comes to your safety. Therefore, the car or utility vehicle you select should:

- Blend in with the environment.
- Have four doors and be roomy enough on the inside to be comfortable.
- Have a powerful engine to get away fast, if necessary.
- Provide great protective bulk.

Any vehicle that is chosen should have the basic conveniences and safety features, i.e., power locks, electronic windows, power steering, antilock brakes, steel-belted radial tires, trunk and hood locks, locking gas cap, and alarm system. The "bulk" of the car increases your ramming and bumping abilities and provides greater mass for crash protection. A powerful engine will improve your getaway abilities.

With a global positioning system (GPS) and cell phones, your company can better stay in touch with you in the event of an emergency. Another system on your vehicle that would be useful is a remote control starter. Besides starting your car to turn on the lights, it can come in handy in the event there is explosive device placed on your vehicle. Most of them are activated when the engine is turned over. You obviously don't want to be sitting inside if a bomb should go off.

Vehicle Design

Realistically, if someone is attacked while in a vehicle, they have a better chance of surviving if they are in a car that is armored. To have this option standard on a vehicle would be very expensive. Unless you are a top-level executive in a large corporation where they are willing to spend the money for your safety, you must do the next best thing and get a vehicle that can withstand an initial attack from kidnappers or terrorists. You will need a vehicle that can:

- Absorb an attack, and take repeated hits to allow you to escape.
- Absorb the initial fire and break the ambush.

In order for you to successfully survive any type of attack while inside your vehicle, it must be two things:

1. Bulky and powerful enough to absorb the initial attack.
2. Maneuverable.

If you are trapped inside a vehicle, you have to be ready to do what it takes to escape. It would be a great investment to do some role-playing. Think about how many different situations you could possibly fall into and begin devising ways to get out of them. (Evasive maneuvers will be discussed shortly.) If the car cannot move because it is blocked in, then use it as a battering ram. The goal is to get away. There can be guns shooting, explosions, and kidnappers coming after you, but *have a plan,* stay focused, and do whatever it will take to get away and stay safe.

Reacting to a Vehicle Attack

If you have a good prevention program you won't have to use the reaction part of your vehicle safety program; it's always better to be safe than sorry. However, attacks happen. Terrorists rely on taking complete control by way of a surprising and vicious assault. Their goal is to kill or neutralize any defenses you may have, and shock you into a submissive mind-set.

During the beginning of an attack, you will initially be fearful, and it is possible to be caught off guard. This is normal. If, however, you haven't had any training such as defensive driving, or even done any mental and physical role-playing, the odds are against you. The big difference between whether or not you become a victim will always be how you respond to the situation. This is why you should start planning *now* and plan on staying in control.

In order to recognize an attack and react, be mindful of the following:

- In order to detect a possible hazardous situation, you must *stay alert at all times* and in all circumstances. *I cannot stress this point enough.* If you have any doubts about your situation, call for assistance, or try to drive somewhere to get assistance.
- Look for any unusual activity such as: a truck blocking the road; a pretty girl who is standing in front of what seems to be an accident; a repair crew that does not seem to be working; cars or trucks with several occupants parked by the road; or unusual inactivity such as streets deserted at the wrong time of the day.
- Be alert to activity and to the road itself, for two or three blocks ahead.

- Always be alert to possible tailing vehicles by using the rearview mirrors.
- Be overly cautious and alert when approaching side streets, roads, access ramps, service roads, and underpasses, as they are prime attack points for kidnappers.
- If possible, do not drive through deserted areas. This would be a perfect place for kidnappers or terrorists to stage an attack.
- Avoid traveling late at night. If it is necessary for a social event, travel with another party.
- Keep an adequate maneuvering distance, using the lane nearest the center of the road.
- The vehicle should always be driven at normal speeds and always under control.
- If attacked, do not leave your vehicle; it should be thought of as a defensive shield, and can also be used as an attack weapon for evasive action.

Possible Evasive Actions

As you read this next section, understand that the evasive maneuvers outlined here should only be attempted if you have had some evasive vehicle training by a professional. Please, don't try these techniques unless you have been trained. *They can be very dangerous.*

Here are some helpful tips for evasive maneuvers:

- If you are being chased, use quick unsignaled turns onto side streets to get away. This is why you should become as familiar as possible with the area you're staying in.
- If they are behind you, use sharp and repeated swerves to the right or left, then stop quickly, which will force the attacker to take defensive action.
- As an alternative move, if they are beside you, repeat the swerves left to right, then stop quickly, causing the attacker to overshoot your car and permit you to make a swift escape from that area of danger.

- While traveling on the freeway at a high speed, cut across the lanes of traffic and make an exit.
- After going around a blind curve, make a bootlegger's turn and take off in the opposite direction.
- After turning a corner, pull over and park. Most of the time the drivers following you are paying attention to what is going on in front of them (and won't notice you on the side of the street.)
- Run a red light or drive the wrong way on a one-way street.

These are just a few techniques used to shake surveillance or to get away from someone who is chasing you.

Attacking with Your Vehicle

Using your vehicle as a weapon will take some nerve and skill, but if you are trying to get away from a group of kidnappers or terrorists, overcoming your nervousness is crucial. You must use your vehicle both as a weapon and a means of escape.

The technique I am outlining here is called ramming. Only do this as a last resort. If you know that you will be responsible for your own driving while in an area of concern, it would be to your advantage to take some training at a defensive driving school. You can never be too safe, and again, it's *always* better to be safe than sorry.

- When you come upon a roadblock, begin slowing down, maintaining a position in the center of the road.
- When you get about twenty-five feet from the roadblock, come to a stop. When your attackers begin to approach you on foot, press the accelerator to top speed and hit as many ambushers as possible.
- When using your vehicle to strike another, make sure it is a controlled crash, striking at a selected point, such as slightly behind the rear or front wheels; continue to accelerate, pushing blocking cars out of the way.

- When dealing with a double vehicle blockade, follow the same process as dealing with a single blockade except strike the blockade in the middle and keep the accelerator down through the collision. Your speed should be between 15 and 30 mph.
- Always be sure that you can generate the necessary speed to make a strike with your vehicle effective.
- In order to maintain control of your vehicle, brace yourself in your seat, keeping your hands on the steering wheel at the eleven and one o'clock positions. Spread your legs with your left leg braced against the door.
- You must have the ability to "clip" a slow moving or stalled vehicle. This is when you attempt to strike an attacker's vehicle on the extreme corner, or at the wheel. Try to strike at a forty-five-degree angle.
- Surprise the attacker by a quick maneuver or by braking to open a gap between the vehicles, then by ramming. The strike will make it difficult for gunmen to fire and it often immobilizes their car. This may provide enough time to escape.
- When an attacker is driving up next to your vehicle, the best way to stop them is by running them off the road. Do this by using your vehicle to press against the front corner of the attacking vehicle. Use the total body weight of your vehicle against the smaller portion of the other vehicle. By using this method, a smaller vehicle can force a much larger one off the road.
- A common method of assassination is for an attacker to pull up alongside the victim's car and shoot everyone inside. The best defense against this attack is to step on the brakes, and cause the attacker to overshoot your vehicle. You can then ram them off the road, or do a bootlegger's turn and make a getaway.

Never give up! Even if you are surrounded, they still have to get out of the vehicle to get to you. You should take this time to ram through them and get away. You have to develop a survival attitude. Violent criminals and terrorists almost always kill their victims, so *never, ever give up when attacked.*

Vehicle Protection

As an executive, you will want to take extra precautions concerning the security of the vehicle that you are driving. If someone targeting you feels it is too risky to get to you out in the open, or it is too hard to figure out your schedule, the next best thing they can do that has been successful in the past is to plant explosives, or a "car bomb." This dangerous weapon can be placed in a vehicle set to explode and destroy a target near the car, or to destroy the vehicle and its occupants.

It is nearly impossible to be fully protected against a car bomb by its very nature, but there are counter-measures which can reduce your chances of becoming a victim. Remember, if you don't have a driver or chauffeur, you may be solely responsible for your own safety.

Here are some tips to help ensure the safety of your vehicle:

- Whenever you park your car, make sure the parking area is strictly controlled, not only by security personnel but also by fencing. The parking lot should also be well lit and patrolled.
- If you are going to dinner or out for the night, don't park anywhere that will leave your vehicle unattended.
- Make sure your vehicle has an alarm system. Make sure the alarm can safeguard the doors, trunk, hood, and the lock on the hood and gas cap.
- You should always have no less than a half tank of gas.
- Planning various routes makes it easier to coordinate avoidance patterns within your overall protection plan.
- Get to know the territory between your workplace and hotel; acquaint yourself with the locations of police, fire, and service stations. This also gives you some familiarity

with side streets and roads which may be necessary to take for evasive action.

Dealing with Car Bombs

If you are concerned about the possibility that a bomb has been placed in your vehicle, then conduct your own search of the vehicle. As a rule of thumb, whenever your vehicle has been out of your control (used by someone else) for a period of time, it should be inspected before being entered, started, or driven.

Vehicle Inspection Procedures

1. The inspection should begin with a survey of the area surrounding the vehicle. Make sure to pay particular attention to bits of wire or string, which may indicate that the car has been tampered with while unattended.
2. Look for dried dirt, which may have been dislodged from beneath the vehicle.
3. After you have checked the area around the vehicle, start inspecting the exterior of the vehicle without touching anything. Pay attention to any misalignment of the doors, windows, trunk lid, and the hood.
4. Also, carefully inspect the engine compartment, gas tank, exhaust and muffler system, wheel wells and wheel covers.
5. Check the vehicle's interior by looking through the windows. Make sure there has been no tampering.
6. After examining the interior from the outside, the car should be entered from the passenger's side and the interior checked. Special attention should be given to the area underneath the dashboard and the seats. Any hanging wire harnesses, or unidentified wires leading to the ignition and hood release, may indicate the presence of a car bomb.
7. If at any time during this inspection something does not feel right, you should immediately stop the inspection and call in the police and bomb experts.

Hotel Safety for Executives

When dealing with hotel safety as an executive, you would take the same precautions as any regular traveler *(refer to chapter Eight: Hotel and Motel Safety)*. Because the nature of an executive and his or her concerns for safety, you must take extra precautions when staying in a hotel, especially a foreign one. Checking in under an assumed name and avoiding rooms on the ground floor (because you are more vulnerable to an attack there than in rooms on the upper levels) are common sense rules for most executives. But be aware that someone could be keeping an eye on you and waiting for you to get careless. In a hotel, there are several opportunities for someone to go after an executive. If you go in with safety and prevention in mind, you will have a better chance of averting a potential kidnapping or terrorist act. Here are some things you can do that will put the odds in your favor.

Meeting with the Hotel Manager

Hotels need business, and they know that if customers are happy with their service, there is a good chance they will get repeat business and the business of your friends and/or associates. When arriving at a new hotel, meet with the hotel manager and get to know him or her. If you tell the manager your concerns about safety, he or she will be able to give some insight into the hotel, the area around it, and the right people to go to for help.

Here are some important things to learn from the hotel manager:

- Location of rooms and floor preference (remember risks, such as fire.)
- Room numbers
- Billing arrangements
- Name of maître d'
- Name of bell captain

- Special events during visit
- Requirements of room and maid services
- Name of the Hotel Security Director

The next person to meet with would be the hotel security director. Find out what he or she has at their disposal and how he or she can best help in case of an emergency. How many guards do they have working on any given shift? Are there security cameras around the hotel, or a security system that can contact the police or fire department if needed? Most of the larger hotel chains take their security seriously and will offer the support needed to help keep people safe.

Other important things to learn from the security director are as follows:

- Any potential problems during your visit.
- Problems encountered in the past (i.e., room thefts, car thefts, pickpockets, fires).
- Location of the safe deposit box.
- Twenty-four-hour security telephone.
- Specific security needs.
- Nature of the armed or unarmed security.
- Local crime index.

Meeting with the Doorman

- Learn his/her name.
- Request that the doorman have your car ready when needed.
- Find out about special parking for VIP's vehicles.
- Find out what level of vehicle supervision there is.

Meeting With the Bell Captain

- Learn his/her name.
- Find out who is directly responsible for handling luggage and getting it to and from your room safely.

Hotel Room Safety Tips

- The best type of room to have is one by the end of the hall, where there is likely to be the least amount of traffic.
- Get a room between the second and eighth floor. This is high enough that intruders could not easily crawl through the windows, but low enough so in case of a fire, the fire department ladders can still reach.
- When in the room, keep the door locked at all times. Also, always keep the "do not disturb" sign on the door, even when the room is not occupied. Keeping the TV on while not in the room will throw off potential burglars.
- Be suspicious of any unusual calls to the room, and do not admit anyone into the room without knowing who they are.
- Lock up anything of value in the hotel safe in your room or at the front desk. Never leave important papers, passports, credit cards, or other valuables out in the open or unattended in the hotel room. Lock up all valuables and extra cash in a hotel safe deposit box.
- Never leave the balcony door open, especially while sleeping. The room could be accessed from other balconies. Use the air conditioner if the room is hot.
- Consider purchasing a portable door alarm. This will at least warn of a possible intrusion and allow a quick reaction.
- Beware of electronic eavesdropping in the room or on the phone. This problem is very common in other countries, to steal information from top businessmen and women from the U.S. Be careful about what is said or to whom information is given when you are in the room or on the phone, unless someone has come in and performed a "sweep" of your room and phone.

Mail Screening Procedures

Here are some things to look for when receiving mail at the hotel:

- Foreign mail and special delivery.
- Restrictive markings (confidential, personal, etc.).
- Excessive postage.
- Poor writing, sloppy typing, or unusual handwriting style.
- The use of an incorrect title or titles.
- Misspelled names or words.
- Oily stains on the envelope or package.
- No return address.
- Extremely heavy, rigid, or thick envelope.
- Lopsided or uneven envelope.
- Unevenly distributed weight.
- Wires or foil protruding from the envelope.
- Extreme amounts of masking tape or string on the envelope.
- Mail with an unusual odor.
- Sealed enclosure within the outer mailing envelope.

These precautions should be taken at home, at the office, or when traveling. If a suspicious looking package is encountered, don't touch or move it. Leave the area and notify the authorities.

Staying Safe During Social Time

When out socializing during leisure time, you may be taking some off time from the job but that doesn't mean you can relax. The bad guys are definitely not taking time off. If they have not yet been able to reach their target, they are hoping that the intended victim will become more laidback during this time and start to make some mistakes on which they can capitalize. When in social situations, there are rules you should abide by to insure your safety.

In a public place such as a restaurant, especially somewhere well known and frequented by foreigners, sit at a table away from the entrance, so you cannot be seen through the front window or door. The goal is to be out of the line of fire and protected from a bomb blast. If there are shots being fired, or there is a bomb blast, then take cover. Get behind something that is solid if possible and get down low. If there is another exit, immediately plan how to get to it safely.

If in a country where kidnapping or terrorism is a possibility, don't ever go anywhere out in public by yourself. Try to stay close and eat in a restaurant in the hotel with other people. When you go outside of the hotel—to a restaurant, show, or event—go with a group of people. There is safety in numbers.

Don't let the hotel staff or the office know your schedule or plans in advance. That information should be restricted to one's family, those traveling with you, and the customer/client/host. The more people who know the schedule, the greater the chance it can get into the wrong hands.

An executive must be very careful when visiting adult entertainment districts. There is a high probability of trouble when catering to bars, strip clubs, etc. There are people whose main business is to set up and rob executives who have too much to drink and get careless. If you *must* go to such an establishment, never go alone. It would be best to have some professional bodyguards or at least someone who knows the area and has some "pull" in this type of situation.

Don't trust anyone. Be wary of anyone who is trying to be your friend. Yes, you will meet all kinds of people when traveling, and most of them are just trying to be friendly. Unfortunately, the bad guys don't wear signs, so be very careful who you socialize with and how much information you give about yourself.

Dealing with Surveillance While on Foot

As with driving, someone can also keep tabs on while you are out and about during social time. While walking, if you suspect that you are being followed, try one of the following tactics.

- Drop something, and when reaching down to pick it up, look behind to see who is following.

- Walk into a building and then turn around abruptly and see if the person following can be identified as someone that you have seen more than once in a short amount of time.
- Board buses, subways, or trains at the last possible moment.
- Look into a shop window for the reflection of the tail (who may stop when you do).
- Alter your appearance by ducking into a store and removing your coat, carrying it over your arm.
- Walk into a building and take the elevator up, then immediately take another elevator down a few flights, staggering your journey to the ground floor in several elevators if possible.

Black Widow: The Female Assassin/Terrorist/Extortionist

Picture this situation. A top executive for a huge corporation meets an attractive woman (this scenario is also possible for female executives, but is more likely with men) in his hotel bar one evening after another long day at their overseas office. After speaking with her for over an hour, he realizes that they have many things in common. They both like to laugh, enjoy opera music, and cannot stand the Boston Red Sox. It's almost like they're old friends.

After a few drinks, he is relaxed and feeling good about himself after a successful day of troubleshooting at the office, so he asks her if she would like to come up to his suite. He figures, "What do I have to lose?" He is in another country. No one will find out—especially his wife or anyone at the home office. So when she says yes, they both get up to leave.

As they're heading out the door, two men in dark suits wearing shades and wearing earpieces stop him. He pulls them over to the side as the young lady waits; they are his bodyguards. He has instructed them to stay in the hotel, but this means they will be in an adjoining room for the rest of the night. The executive has been traveling with security for the last five years without incident and feels good about their track record. The bodyguards agree to come up after he escorts his lady friend to his room.

As the executive and his lady friend are going up in the elevator, she starts to kiss him. As they are hot in embrace, she suggests that they should go to her room where they won't have to worry about anyone disturbing them; she says that she would be very uncomfortable knowing someone is in the next room with access while they are enjoying themselves. He gives in, and they go to her room. They have a great night, so he thinks.

The next morning, after getting her phone number and saying their goodbyes, the executive heads back to his room. His bodyguards are already waiting there, understandably worried. It's their job to protect him and know where he is at all times, and they did neither. Seeing them shaken, the executive tries to reassure them that they don't have to worry about their jobs. No one has to know about this incident.

A week after coming home, the CEO of the company asks the executive to have an emergency meeting with him. Being the golden boy of the company, the executive thinks he's getting another pat on the back by the boss for another job well done.

As he walks in, he sees they are not alone. He knows the four attorneys and head of security that are already seated, but has no idea who the other people are. With a forced smile, he walks over to his boss and greets him with a handshake, asking, "What's up, boss? Who are all these new people?"

After his boss takes a hard look at him, he is told to sit down. The CEO asks him one question, "Did you meet anyone while you were out of town last week?"

Of course, the executive says, "No."

Then the CEO takes a TV-VCR remote control and turns on the television. Film of him making love to the woman he met last week appears onscreen. The CEO asks, "Who were you with while you were on your business trip?"

The executive meekly tells his boss how he met this woman and what they did, knowing this is going to be trouble. When he's done, the CEO begins to introduce everyone else in the room, including two FBI men standing in the rear of the room.

The CEO proceeds to tell the executive that not only is he in trouble, but because of his lack of judgment, he has put the company in an uncompromising position. His boss reveals that the executive has been set up for blackmail. The woman was given all the information on him and was paid very well to get him in bed. A pro, she understands the psychology of a successful man with power and what makes him tick. She was smart enough to get him to go to her room, where secret cameras were set up by people in the next room filming the whole night. There are also still pictures of him getting cozy with the woman while in the bar. They have the goods on him, and everything he has worked for over the years (family, job, and reputation) is on the line.

The blackmailers knew he was the "golden boy" of this particular corporation and that the company, with such a clean reputation, couldn't afford to have a scandal like this. Unofficially, the FBI agents (who are actually friends with the CEO) recommend they should secretly pay the blackmail ransom so there isn't any public humiliation to the company.

After the ransom is paid and everything about the incident dies down, our superstar executive takes a forced early retirement, goes through a nasty divorce, and is never able to get back to where he was in the past.

This story is based on the lives of several executives and the uncompromising situations in which they placed themselves and their companies. The common mistake anyone in this position makes is they think something like this can ever happen to them. You have to remember the rules—if you are not aware, a smart woman can take even the savviest man out of his game plan and make him do things that he would never dream of doing. The use of a woman to infiltrate the infrastructures of even the most protected man has been done since the beginning of time. The problem is that the executive, who is supposed to be protected, starts to change the very rules that were made to keep him safe. He gets so caught up in the situation that he forgets to adhere to basic precautions like checking into her background to see if she is indeed who she says she is, or finding out if she is there for the reason she claims to be. Answering these two questions will tell you a lot.

The other mistake he makes is to be alone with a woman he has just met or has only known for a short time. He doesn't know her true intentions. In order to "get his groove on," he takes a chance with his reputation and maybe his life. If he has bodyguards, he has prevented them from doing their job of protecting him. There really is no win-win in this situation except maybe for the woman.

The average man has never been with a movie star-beautiful woman. Have you ever watched a group of men when a pretty woman is present? The majority of them go crazy. When this group of men speaks within their inner circle, bragging about what they would do if they had the chance to be with that woman, they all know the truth within themselves. They wouldn't know what to do if they were in the room with her alone. They don't have the tools or believe they are worthy to have a knockout beauty.

The one thing that every successful executive has is power and money. This draws both men and women to them. The challenge any man of power has is to say "No" to the thousands of temptations he has to deal with everyday. Movie stars, professional athletes, and politicians are bombarded with numerous temptations which can get them into trouble. The top executives and CEOs of many well-known corporations have become as famous and as well known as rock stars. This means anyone who has the resources can find out anything they need to set this type of person up and use this information against them; but they must first get to you and put you in a situation that will put them in control.

Here are the three main reasons to "set-up" an executive:

1. Blackmail
2. Kidnapping
3. Assassination

The reasons why are too numerous to get into, but believe me, these situations happen more than people would like to admit. Your job is to not become a victim who falls prey to one of them. The following are some things men must learn if they are to understand how to deal with women when it comes to their safety.

Any trained woman can be just as dangerous as a man, both mentally and physically. But they have one more weapon they can use on a heterosexual man that men don't have: their sexuality. Given the right circumstances, a smart and experienced woman can push the hot buttons and make someone do things they wouldn't normally do given the right circumstances.

The main thing a "black widow" needs to know is where you will be. This information is so vital in order to complete their task. The best place for a woman to catch an executive and spin her web is during his down time when he is relaxed, sociable, and drinking. Places such as hotel bars, lobbies, restaurants, dance clubs, and casinos are most typical.

I've heard stories from bodyguard friends whose clients were just sitting down in a bar having drinks, when women came over and started talking to them and being very friendly; out of nowhere the women began sitting on their laps. All of the businessmen were married and had no intentions of fooling around. After several attempts, the ladies still couldn't persuade the men to have any fun with them. When the men got back to the main office the next week, someone had sent pictures of them to the big dogs, with the women sitting on their laps. Even though they didn't do anything, the pictures taken of them tell a different story. They ended up having to pay off the blackmailer to save the company from an embarrassing incident.

Especially if you are by yourself, if you leave with a woman and go wherever she wants, she can just as easily set you up for a multitude of other problems. Anything from robbery, kidnapping, and alleged rape to assassination is possible if you are not careful. If you go to her room, it may be wired for sound, camera, or someone can be waiting for you once she gets you inside. She can drug your drink when you aren't looking.

Remember, the worst thing you can do is go with someone by yourself. If you are a top executive, male or female, you must remain alert to influences that would place you in harm's way.

Kidnappings

Executives working for large corporations and traveling for business overseas are more likely to be candidates for a kidnapping. Mexico and Colombia have the largest number of people kidnapped every year, but the numbers that are available are not accurate because most kidnappings are never reported, and, as mentioned earlier, nobody really wants you to know how many people are missing each year.

Top-level executives are prime targets for kidnappings because there are large insurance policies on them. This means there will be a huge payoff; usually, the corporation in question will be contacted, and negotiations for a release will be worked out. If the kidnappers get their ransom money, there is a good chance of the executive being released. If not, the executive's safety becomes a roll of the dice and anything can happen.

If all the preventative measures have been followed and an executive still falls prey to a kidnapping, it was because of carelessness and predictability. The assailants were able to keep track of the subject and planned the time and place to abduct him or her. Once kidnapped, a victim is usually blindfolded, gagged, and tied up. The captors will take them somewhere low-key and out of the way, preferably without windows. They will then show proof that they have the victim either by recorded message by phone, or with a picture of the victim with the day's newspaper. The captors send it to the negotiators, and the waiting game begins.

Remember, the victim is only valuable to the captors alive, and they want to keep him or her that way.

The following are a few rules for surviving a kidnapping:

1. The first thing to do is think positively. Only then can you focus on getting out of the situation alive.
2. Force yourself to stay cool and calm. Keep a passive attitude. Attempting to resist or becoming violent at this time could cause you to be seriously injured or killed.
3. Try to establish a rapport with the kidnappers.
4. Plan on being held captive for a while.
5. Maintain dignity and self-respect at all times.
6. Try to maintain good physical and mental health. Eat the food they offer and try to exercise. Exercising helps one to stay relaxed.
7. Keep the mind active. If allowed, read and write as much as possible.
8. Take mental notes of the kidnappers and the surroundings: their characteristics, speech, habits, and things like distinctive sounds from outside. This information could prove very valuable later.
9. If questioned, keep the answers short. Don't volunteer information.
10. If there is truly a chance to escape, do so. If under a threat of death or being shot, *don't* try to escape.
11. If an assault force is sent in for rescue, stay calm and stay out of the way. Find a safe spot to drop down to or hide behind. Stay there and be still until the action is over. If you make any sudden moves, you could be mistaken for one of the kidnappers and shot.

Percentage-wise, tourists don't have to worry as much as a big-time executive when it comes to kidnapping. The problem for a tourist is, if he or she decides to journey to a remote region, say one that is known as a drug area, they are at a higher risk of becoming kidnapped. To be safe, it is always best to thoroughly investigate any proposed vacation destination.

Pick five ways a business executive can be safer when traveling abroad on a business trip:

1.

2.

3.

4.

5.

Chapter Thirteen

Staying "Street Smart" in Unfamiliar Cities

One sure thing when traveling is Murphy's Law: "Anything that can go wrong, will go wrong."

Over the years of traveling, I have had my share of adventures. There have been several close calls, and by the grace of the Man upstairs, I am still here. One of these close calls happened in the late nineties in Los Angeles while I was working on a movie. I also had to do a voice-over for a series of self-defense videos that were shot earlier in the year. I was killing two birds with one stone while staying in LA. After a day of taping, a guy on staff was taking me back to where I was staying, but he really had no idea where he was going. As we drove toward the street we were looking for, we took a shortcut down another street that had a familiar name. That was the wrong move.

We had just driven into a Mexican *barrio*. As soon as the guys from this neighborhood saw us, they knew we didn't belong there. As they came off stairs and stoops, we sped down the street to make a hasty getaway. Unfortunately, our getaway was short-lived—about half a block down there was a dead end, with a high fence that overlooked a canal.

I wasn't driving, so I had to direct and guide my driver. The first thing I had to do was to get him to turn the car around. Understandably, he was frantic. My heart was beating a hundred miles an hour, but I was cool and calm. I knew there were decisions that had to be made pretty fast. As the crowd started to rush toward us, my driver stopped the car and asked, "What should we do?"

I could see baseball bats, axes, and an entire assortment of weapons in the hands of the people in the crowd. I screamed to the man driving, "Step on the gas now!" He was still in shock and would not react so I reached over and stepped on the gas with his foot under mine. Everything happened so fast. As we sped through the crowd there were bodies jumping and flying out of the way, and at the same time we could hear and see the car being struck over and over as we made our getaway. It was like a scene from the movie *Escape from LA*. As we whipped around the corner speeding, I still had my foot all the way down on the gas for about a block before I let up on it.

We were both quiet as we drove down the street looking for a familiar landmark, and ten minutes later, we finally pulled up to the right place. As I got out of the car, I made a joke about "Let's do this again sometime," but he was not laughing. I thanked him for the ride, and as he pulled away, I could see under the lights how much damage was done to the car. It looked like Swiss cheese. There were chopped holes, dents, scrapes, and cracked windows.

I never saw or heard from this man again, but this incident made me more aware of how important it is to know where you are going, and the best way to get there, ahead of time. When traveling to unfamiliar cities, it can make the difference between life and death.

Staying Safe While Vacationing and Traveling

Whatever accommodations one selects, vacationers will most likely go sight-seeing, shopping and out to eat. In order to ensure your safety, you must use the same common sense as you would if in the USA. Vacationers must especially be cautious and avoid areas where they can likely be a victim.

Safety on the Streets

- Don't take shortcuts in narrow alleys or on poorly lit streets.
- Avoid public demonstrations and other disturbances.
- Be wary of people who suddenly want to become friendly. Never discuss travel plans or other personal matters with someone.
- Learn a few phrases in the local language to signal someone when in need of help or directions and for basic communication.
- Avoid scam artists offering bargains or to be a guide.
- If possible, don't travel at night; if you do, take a companion.
- Even when lost, act as if you know where you are going. Only ask for directions from someone of authority.

How to Carry Yourself and Be Aware of Your Surroundings

The number one rule when on the streets is to be aware and not distracted. Here are some things to remember:

- Before venturing out in public, ask someone at the front desk for directions if you are unsure of how to reach your destination. Avoid looking or acting like a tourist. Walking around constantly taking pictures or looking at a map will be a dead giveaway that someone is not a local.
- Walk and talk with a sense of purpose and confidence.
- Make eye contact when passing someone, and scan the area from time to time.
- If alone and passing anything or anyone that causes nervousness, trust your instincts. Stop and let that person

pass, or walk into a public place. If coming up on a situation that causes nervousness, turn around and go the other way, or cross the street.
- Avoid going down isolated streets and alleys alone. If possible, walk down the middle of the sidewalk facing traffic.
- Always stay alert. Daydreaming or window-shopping makes you a prime target.
- Never take your money out in public.
- Never overload yourself with shopping bags or packages. Take a cab if necessary.
- Never buy anything from someone off the street. Nine times out of ten, the tourists will come out the loser in the purchase.
- If jogging, never do so in isolated places. Always stay focused, and never do anything that can be distracting, like wearing headphones while running.
- If followed, glance back to acknowledge that someone is there and then make a conscious decision on what to do next; don't do "nothing." If possible, go to a public place and have them call the police.
- Don't get caught up into thinking most crimes only happen at night. Most people let their guard down in the daytime by thinking nothing can happen to them, and that is when they are usually caught by surprise.

Having a Buddy System

When going out of town, it is always a good idea to have a friend to do things with and depend upon. It's also great from a safety perspective. When out in public, the bad guys prefer to target someone alone. Handling one person is much easier than trying to handle several. You should like being with this person, and even more importantly, it should be someone trustworthy. This person must take safety as seriously as you do.

Don't Look or Act Like a Tourist

The biggest mistake people make when they are out of town is they look like they don't belong. In this situation one might as well tie a sign around their neck that says, "Take advantage of me." When out of town, people want to enjoy themselves, not become a victim of crime that could have been avoided.

Given below are a few tips on staying safe in foreign streets:

- Never dress in a way that will cause attention. You want to blend in with your surroundings, not become the center of attention. Don't dress to be sexy or wear expensive clothes. Dress to be comfortable. Someone is always watching and waiting for his or her next victim. Don't become the next statistic.
- Never carry a camera or look at a map while out in public. This will definitely bring attention, and make you look like a tourist. Remember, when in doubt, take a picture with your mind.
- If traveling for a convention, never wear an ID badge out in public, or carry anything that will connect you with the convention. This is a dead giveaway that you are out of town.

Protecting Your Money or Valuables

The common perception is that most American tourists carry a lot of money, and if robbed they won't be around to identify or testify against the robbers should they be caught. This is why it is so important to not look or act like a victim while in public and or traveling. When traveling for either business or pleasure, most people are not thinking about their safety or even protecting their belongings. But to minimize the chances of becoming a victim of these types of crimes, follow certain safety rules to prevent from becoming a victim.

Here are some useful tips that can help make any trip a safer one:

- Never go out of town with valuable jewelry or a lot of cash. Wearing/carrying it may make one feel good, but remember, there is always someone watching, and they may have chosen you as their next victim.
- This is worth repeating: *never* carry large amounts of cash. It is just asking for trouble. If carrying a large amount, separate your funds. Never put all of your money in one place when you're going to be out in public. Hide it on different parts of the body like inside shoes or socks, a coat pocket, or carry a money belt to hide your cash. Remember to never carry more than you are willing to lose. Besides hiding the money, be ready to have enough money to give away if you do happen to be robbed. Sometimes it is a lot easier to give your assailant something rather than to try to prevent the crime, especially if you have never trained in any type of self-defense.
- Keep anything of value out of sight and in inconspicuous containers. If you will be leaving something of value in the car, then put it in the trunk, but don't do it while anyone is watching.
- If leaving something of value in a car, never leave it overnight. Also, don't leave anything in a trunk while parked in an isolated area.
- Never take public transportation, especially buses or trams, after getting large amounts of cash at the bank. Get the money back to the hotel safe and take just what is needed for the day.
- When going out for the day, only take what you need for the particular trip. Don't take your passport, multiple credit cards, most of the money, and traveler's checks. Just take what you need for the day and lock the rest up in the hotel safe.

Purse Safety

Purse-snatching has become one of the easiest crimes to commit. Because so many women carry a purse and often have their money inside, this crime can happen anytime or anywhere. The one thing the purse snatcher or thief has on his side is that most victims are too caught up in their own world to always be thinking about their purse. When he decides who his victim is going to be, he has also already planned his escape. Once the wheels are in motion, there is a good chance of committing the crime and getting away. This is why one *must* stay alert when out on the streets.

Here are some helpful tips to help you hold on to your purse:

- When in public, always keep your purse with you at all times. Never set it down unless you can keep an eye on it.
- Keep the purse firmly under your arm, with the flap side toward your body. If you let the purse just hang or dangle, it will be easier for someone to run up and snatch it.
- Have a strong grip on the purse strap in case someone tries to take it, but you have to decide, "If this ever happens to me, at what point am I willing to give up my purse?" There are some criminals who are willing to drag their victims on the ground or even cut the purse strap with a knife and cut them in the process, if they don't let go of the purse during the robbery.
- When wearing a coat, carry the purse under the coat.
- When walking down the street, watch for purse-snatchers on bikes or motorcycles and in passing cars.
- When sitting down in a public place, i.e., a restaurant, or even in the restroom, always keep your purse in your lap or between your legs.

Remember to never leave anything in a purse that can't be replaced. If this crime happens, nothing is worth your life. Use your head. Money and lipstick are replaceable, but your life is not.

Watching Out for Scams and Con Games

There are so many scams and con games out there that I could write a book on this subject by itself. In order to keep safe and out of trouble, let's focus on the scams most likely to be encountered while traveling. Understand that there are people who make a living taking items of value from others. These thugs train for years, some actually going to an unofficial school, training in a particular scam or con.

Distraction Scams

This crime often requires something as simple as a bump or dropping something, to more elaborate distractions such as staging a heart attack. Here are things to look out for so as not to become a victim of this crime.

- The quickest way to lose something is to set it down. If the item has any value, don't take your eyes off it for a second or the item will be gone.
- Don't be fooled by a stranger who appears to be overly friendly or helpful. This may sound a little too cautious, but this could be a distraction to set innocent people up for a crime.
- Some con artists and pickpockets work in twos and sometimes in threes to better set their victims up. It could be a woman distracting a man, or a child distracting a woman.
- When at the airport or a hotel checking in or out, never take your eyes off your luggage.
- You shouldn't wear expensive jewelry or watches in public, but if you do, be aware of the surroundings.

- Men should keep their wallet in a front inside pocket. Never in the back pocket (which also causes back problems).
- Never underestimate or trust anyone who is a stranger.

It doesn't matter where you may be—in a five-star hotel, in an airport, or just shopping—you always must be aware of the surroundings. This also means maintaining physical possession of one's belongings and keeping an eye on them at all times.

Con Artists and Street Hustlers

These kinds of criminals are street smart and understand human nature. They know that the average person is greedy and likes to get something for nothing. The job is to capitalize from greed, and these hustlers do very well to that end. The first thing con artists do is gain your trust. Once they do that, the scam is to get their victims to put up their own money as a sign of "good faith." One can say, "This could never happen to me," but crimes like these can and do happen to the most intelligent people all the time. Greed makes us do strange things, but remember, "You can't get something for nothing." Here are some rules to live by when dealing with suspected con artists and street hoods.

1. Don't ever think a hustler can be hustled. If the story sounds too good to be true, it probably is.
2. If he or she wants to play a game or bet for money, don't do it. Most likely they will let you win the first few times to build up their victim's confidence and then win more money on a larger bet.
3. Avoid buying anything from street vendors or hustlers. Anything bought off the street is a big risk, and there is the chance of being "taken."
4. Never take a wallet out on the street. Someone is always watching, and that may not be a good thing.

The best thing to combat these types of street crimes is not to be sucked into anything that doesn't seem right. It's worth repeating: stay alert, and be aware of your surroundings.

ATM Safety

ATM's have become one of the most popular targets of crime today. First, it's easy to assume that people are there to obtain cash, and second, there is a lack of security. This makes this crime difficult to deal with. If using an ATM machine, be aware of the surroundings at all times, and try to get the cash during the day.

Given below are some safety tips when using the ATM:

- When possible, never go alone to use the ATM machine to make a deposit or a withdrawal.
- Use an ATM that is located in a supermarket, convenience store, or drive through. These places are well lit and populated.
- Reduce the chances of being robbed by using an ATM machine during the day.
- When using an outside ATM, don't use one that is in an isolated area.
- When you arrive at an ATM machine, scan the area first, and if you don't like what you see or if someone makes you feel uncomfortable, do not stop.
- Don't always assume that a person standing in front of the ATM machine is legitimate. They could be there to set you up. Even if they are there to use the machine, give them space until they finish their transaction.
- While using the ATM machine, stay alert to the surroundings, scanning them as you make your transaction.
- When entering your pin number, use your body as a shield in case someone is trying to look over your shoulder during your transaction.
- When finished, be sure to take the card and receipt and leave immediately. Avoid counting it, or flashing large amounts of cash.

Don't underestimate the possibility of crime in this location. Skimming, the use of video and photo cameras from a distance, and taking advantage of people who forget to clear their pin number have all been used against unsuspecting victims. Don't get caught in this situation. *Be aware.*

Dealing with Panhandlers

This situation is more annoying than anything else. Most panhandlers are harmless, but they can make people uncomfortable. Here are a few tips that can make your life easier when dealing with panhandlers:

- Never feel obligated to give them money.
- When giving money to a panhandler, have coins or bills ready. Never open your purse or wallet in public.
- If a panhandler becomes verbally louder and aggressive, walk away immediately.
- Don't be drawn into a verbal or physical confrontation.

The main thing to remember: do not feel intimidated into giving money. Always give because you want to, not because you feel obligated or afraid.

Shopping Safety

Shopping is fun, but one should still be alert and aware of what is going on around them. Here are some tips to make shopping safer.

- Never flash large amounts of cash when paying for something. Someone could be watching.
- Women should never lay their purse down. It's easy to walk off and forget it, or someone may try to steal it.
- Don't overdress or wear expensive jewelry, as this can attract unwanted attention.
- Shop with a friend if possible.

- Spend less time protecting expensive items by purchasing them last.
- Don't load yourself down with packages. This will make you an easier target on the streets. If you have a car, put your packages in the trunk and not in the back seat or floor of the car where someone can possibly see and then steal them.

The key is to stay alert and be aware of what is going on around you. Trust your instincts.

Parking Lot Safety

If you are driving, there are certain rules you should follow to maximize your safety when going to and from the car. The ideal parking lot is well lit, with security and a limited number of exits and entrances.

Here are a few tips to keep you safe in a parking lot:

- Park as close as possible to the elevators or stairs leading to the building.
- Always remember where the car is parked (check for row numbers, etc.).
- If you return to the car to drop off packages, move the car to a different part of the parking lot and hide the packages in the trunk.
- When a valet parks the car, only give the ignition key. Keep the keys from your trunk and house. People have been robbed, because they left the house key with their car keys, and a copy was made for later use.
- Also make sure you give the car to a real valet. Check for other matching uniforms if possible. If unverifiable, just drive away.
- When returning to the car in a self-parking lot, don't zigzag between parked cars. Walk down the main roll and stay alert.

How to Approach Your Vehicle

Sometimes we become complacent when going to and from our car, but this is one of the weakest links regarding safety.

Here are a few tips on safely reaching your car:

1. When approaching the car, have keys in hand and scan the area as you get closer. Also, look underneath the vehicle to make sure no one is hiding.
2. If the car has power locks, wait until you're close to the car before unlocking it.
3. Trust your instincts. If anyone is hanging around the car, keep walking or turn around and go back inside when possible.
4. Once close to the car, take a look at your backseat before getting inside to make sure no one is hiding there.
5. Lock your doors once inside.
6. If your car won't start, or has a flat tire, the problem could be deliberate. Scan the area for anything suspicious. If the area appears to be safe, go back inside and call for help or use a cell phone.
7. Be cautious about accepting help from strangers. They could have been the culprits who did the damage.
8. No matter what, don't ever get in the car with an attacker. Statistically, your chances of survival are increased if you don't get in.

If You Are Confronted

When it comes to being a victim of crime, each situation is different. It would be impossible to tell anyone how to handle every single situation that might arise. Because each circumstance is unique, only you can assess your best options. Even if someone is trained in self-defense or has a weapon, there is no guarantee that he or she will come out on top if there is no plan of action. The one thing you can always do to better prepare yourself for this type of situation is to prepare your *mind* in the event a confrontation becomes a reality.

If a confrontation arises and someone wants to relieve you of your possessions, what is your plan of action? First things first: it's best to err on the side of safety. Remember, possessions can be replaced, but a life cannot.

Here are some rules to be followed when confronted by an attacker:

1. If confronted by a robber, the best thing to do is to hand over your money or valuables and anything else they ask for. If you are not trained to defend yourself, try to stay calm and don't resist. Don't argue with him or her, show hostility, make any sudden movements, or stare with steady eye contact. Just because a weapon is not visible, that doesn't mean the attacker doesn't have one. If they are young, they can be even more dangerous. Add to this the fact that they could be high on drugs, nervous, or just plain crazy. Don't risk physical injury.
2. Don't mouth off. This can be a traumatic situation. You must try to remain calm. If the attacker asks anything, listen carefully, and then reply in a calm voice. Remember to avoid making any sudden movements. Inform the robber that you are reaching for something before making a move.
3. After handing over valuables, stay calm until the attacker leaves. You just want this awful incident to end; however, this is when a victim is most valuable to the assailant. Most robbers will just leave with their take, but some will want the victim to come with him or her.
4. If asked to go with the attacker, under no circumstances are you to go! If they try to force you into a car, *the rules have changed.* Even if they have a weapon—run

and scream. It is better to take chances now, than to get in a car where your chances of getting away are slim to none.
5. If you decide to fight back, be mentally prepared to follow through with the attack 110 percent. Fight back with all your heart to stay alive and escape. Once you start fighting back to protect yourself, don't stop until your man (or woman) is down and out. This is why it is so important to take a self-defense class.
6. Try to remember the details about your assailant, such as their height, weight, color of clothing, birthmarks, tattoos, and any other distinguishing characteristics. Also remember, if they drove a car or truck, get the license plate number.
7. Always report a mugging or a robbery to the police, even if you are not hurt or nothing of value was taken.
8. If someone in a car threatens you while running or jogging, turn around and run in the opposite direction from the way the car is driving. Cross the street and run in the opposite direction if possible.
9. When sensing any danger, start running away from the potentially bad situation and start screaming and shouting for someone to call the police or get help. The key is to attract as much attention as possible. If there is any place nearby where there is a crowd, run there and seek assistance.

Unfortunately, the safety tips that are given in this chapter only scratch the surface of what we have to watch out for while vacationing and traveling. When all is said and done, it is up to the individual to be accountable for his or her safety. This starts with the mind-set that again, individuals should *always* be aware of what is going on around them. Then you can take steps to deal with the situation accordingly.

Not long ago, I saw a news report of a gentleman who was on vacation at a casino, won a large sum of money, and was followed back to his hotel and robbed of it. He was too embarrassed to be viewed on camera, so only the back of his head was shown.

He started by saying that he met a fun guy while gambling at the casino, and they hit it off right away. After gambling together for a while, they had a couple of drinks in one of the bars in the casino. They left a short while later and walked out to the parking lot, splitting up to go to their respective cars.

As the gentleman was opening the door to his hotel room, two guys from behind pushed him inside, bound and gagged him, and took his money. He was tied up all night until the cleaning woman came in the next morning and found him.

When the police came to take the report, they came to the conclusion that the man he had befriended at the casino was one of the robbers. The newscaster covering this story went on to say that this is not an isolated incident. It happens quite frequently. An attacker chooses his victim by watching who wins a lot of money, and then he works on trying to befriend him. If he finds the right person willing to be his friend, he can work his "mojo" on him.

Once the unsuspecting person leaves, his newfound friend leaves at the same time. This gives the crook several ways to rob his victim. He can either rob him in the parking lot along with some of his buddies waiting for him outside, or if the parking lot does not work at that time, they will follow him back to his hotel and try to rob him as he is opening the door to his room. Either way, it can get "mean and nasty."

This one situation is just another example of how people can be caught off guard during a time when they are supposed to be relaxing and having a good time. I do not expect people to be on red alert 24-7, but they should develop an attitude of awareness when out, whether for work or for pleasure. By thinking about safety ahead of time, potential victims will have a better chance to handle these situations, because they realized and faced the possibility of an attack.

Pick five ways you can keep yourself safer when you are on the streets:

1.

2.

3.

4.

5.

Chapter Fourteen

Gender—and Age-Specific Travel Safety

Special Tips for Female Travelers

There are certain precautions a woman should take when traveling. Unfortunately, attitudes toward women vary from country to country, and while many of the previous tips apply to women, there are some special tips for them to ensure their safety.

When Shopping

- Never leave a purse unintended in a shopping cart or on a counter.
- When asked for identification, only give the information that is requested. Never surrender your entire wallet or card case.
- Never flash large amounts of money. You should check for your credit card periodically, and immediately report any loss.

When Driving

- Always look inside before entering a car.
- Keep the gas tank full.
- Keep the widows rolled up and the door locked.
- Park in a well-lit area near the destination
- If followed, blow the horn repeatedly to attract attention and drive to a safe spot.
- When abroad and traveling solo, use public transportation whenever possible (subways, trains). Incidents of rape and robbery of lone women in cabs are extremely high.
- Don't keep cameras, purses, etc. out in the open while driving, because there are robbers who will commit the "smash and grab," a crime where they smash windows to steal valuables.
- If the car breaks down, raise the hood and trunk and remain inside with the doors locked and windows rolled up, until the police arrive or help comes because you have called for it.
- Never pick up strangers.
- At night, drive only on well-lit streets, even if it means going out of the way.

When Traveling the Streets

- As a woman, it can be very risky to walk alone, as it can make for an easy target of various crimes. Try to find others to walk with, even for short distances.
- Always walk with a sense of purpose and look and feel confident. Even when lost, try not to look unsure.
- When walking, be alert and scan the premises from time to time.
- Eye contact with strangers can be good or bad depending on the gender, ethnicity, and location one is in. Some groups perceive eye contact as a challenge, while for others it is a display of respect. In other circumstances, eye contact can short circuit trouble, by making you seem confident and in control.

- Walk on well-lit, heavily-traveled streets. Avoid shortcuts through alleys.
- Hold your purse under the arm, with the flap on the inside.
- When walking on the streets, watch out for purse snatchers who work from bikes, motorcycles, and passing cars.
- Keep your hands free. People are more vulnerable when their hands are full of bags and a purse.
- Be willing to be verbal and talk loud, if/when feeling threatened.
- Be prepared to run if followed. If threatened from a car, run in the opposite direction to seek help.
- Dress conservatively.
- If approached by a suspicious person, cross the street or change direction.
- Don't be too quick to get close with someone new to you. More than one person has been tricked, drugged, raped, and even murdered by people they thought they could trust.

When in Buildings

- Use an elevator whenever possible, but stay alert and be aware if a suspicious looking person gets on. Always stand near the control panel, and if a passenger makes a menacing move, hit as many floors' buttons as possible. Don't risk your safety by using a poorly lit stairwell.
- Be very discrete about revealing personal plans to others.
- When using a restroom, chose one that is in a public building or facility. If there is a single restroom that you can lock, this would be your best choice. If not, use the toilet that is closest to the far wall. Never hang your valuables on the hook behind the door. Someone can reach over and take your belongings and escape before you know it. If you must put your purse or valuables on the floor, put them between your legs.

- Always keep your jacket and purse with you. For instance, you would not want to leave your purse in a department store dressing room, when you go looking for more merchandise. Thieves who pose as patrons will exploit this error.
- When out in public, you are always being watched. Handle money with discretion. There are thieves just waiting for someone to pull out large sums of money.
- When in a hotel room, if someone knocks on the door, make sure they identify themselves and request that they tell you why they are there. If this person claims to be from hotel maintenance or to be there to repair your TV set or phone, don't open the door until you have called down to the front desk to make sure he/she is on legitimate business.

Here are more safe tips for women who travel:

- Have a plan. Know what you are doing and where you are going at all times.
- If possible, use the buddy system when going out.
- Stay alert and be aware at all times.
- Do not hitchhike.
- Schedule most of your long distance travel for daytime hours. Don't travel at night when you are most vulnerable.
- Travel lightly.
- Never give out your room number in a hotel. Always meet new acquaintances in the lobby.
- Never tell a stranger your room's telephone number or let anyone in the room without checking with the front desk first.
- When driving anywhere, keep all doors locked.
- Walk against, not with the main flow of traffic when you can.
- Carry a cell phone.
- Always walk and carry yourself with confidence. Make eye contact and be assertive.

- Don't overdress while you are out in public.
- If wearing expensive jewelry, hide it until you reach your destination.
- When carrying a purse, never carry more than you can afford to lose. Store your real valuables in your pocket.
- You don't have to be friendly to strangers.
- Married or not, you should wear a wedding ring. This will not stop the most persistent guy, but it does make most people think twice before trying to pick you up.
- If someone is making unwanted advances, stay strong and let him know you are not interested.
- If you are being verbally harassed, don't respond. Just walk away.
- If you are alone, always let someone you trust know where you are at all times.
- At conventions and seminars, remove your name tag before leaving the facility.
- When possible, let someone know where you are going and when you intend to return.
- Women should avoid rooms with easy access to the outside, especially rooms on the first floor or sliding glass doors.
- Women should not go out alone at night. In some countries, men can become more aggressive with a woman unescorted by a man.

The Night Life

One sure thing is that most young people like to partake in the nightlife when on vacation. Many people are under the impression that the nightlife lures single professionals and married couples, but the largest group of people that like to party are of college age. During spring break and the summer months, many vacation spots around the world are inundated with young college students who sleep late during the day and party all night. As you may well know, the popular thing is for these youngsters to meet someone to "hook up" with and have fun. It's one big game.

The goal: drink, have as much fun as possible, and hopefully meet someone. Then they will go back and tell their friends about a "hot" boy or girl they met, and that it was the greatest vacation they ever had.

Most people who travel to different places around the world to vacation and have a good time partying come away satisfied with the experience. But there is always the other side of the coin. Lately, more and more women are having negative experiences when they are out enjoying the nightlife. Serious crimes have become a problem for young ladies who are just out to have a "good time."

When you are out partying and drinking, you become more uninhibited. You may do things you wouldn't think of doing back home. Case in point, the popular DVD series "Girls Gone Wild" has had commercials running for the last ten years and has sold millions of DVD's. This has made founder Joe Francis a multimillionaire. The whole premise of the DVD is to find young girls on spring break who are out partying and get them to show their breasts and commit other lewd acts, and get them on film. Sadly, the formula works very well. Get a bunch of girls who have been drinking excessively and who just want to let loose and have some fun. When someone comes up and asks them to bare their breasts on camera for a lousy T-shirt, you would think any normal person would just be smart enough to say, "No," but they don't. More and more young ladies fall prey to this situation, only to have returned from that wild weekend and wished there was something they could do to take it back.

You may still be asking, "How can an educated, sensible young lady put herself in such an embarrassing predicament?" Even the most levelheaded adult will do things that they wouldn't normally do in the right mix of circumstances or when under the influence of alcohol. So take a group of college kids going on spring break, after a stressful and grinding year in school, put them in a situation where they are just starting to have some independence, and things can get a little crazy. People start out doing small things that they feel are a little wild, then add some alcohol and get a rush. After a while, with some egging on by friends, youngsters are capable of doing almost anything, because they are having fun, and don't think anybody will find out (or they are so intoxicated that they don't care). The next thing you know, *voilà*, they are on the cover of "Girls Gone Wild."

Now, I'm not saying every young adult is out to get wild and sin the first chance they have some independence, but I'm making a point about how easy it is to get caught up in the moment when you're out having fun and not thinking about the seriousness of your safety. Yes, people will meet other people. This is human nature and will never change. It would be to one's advantage to find out something about the person he/she is interested in before getting serious. There should always be limitations when partying on vacation.

Here are some tips to ensure your safety:

- Don't go out partying alone. Most people do not go out alone in general; the same thing should apply when going out for the night. There is safety in numbers.
- Before leaving, plan your evening ahead of time. Once the rules are decided upon, stick with them. Keep each other honest. Having friends around reduces the chances of someone trying to take advantage of anyone in the group.
- Know your destination before leaving. The goal is to have a good time, but in some places both here and abroad, there are criminals out there who are just waiting for some tourists to make the wrong turn down a side street and get lost. This is exactly what the thugs want. They will rush the unsuspecting tourist's car, point a gun at them, and steal their valuables. In countries such as Mexico or Russia, you could be more than just robbed. Some tourists have been kidnapped and even murdered over the years.
- Have a designated driver. Remember, anytime there is alcohol involved, people do not make the best decisions, not only in terms of watching their backs but also driving

to and from destinations. Drunk driving is a serious crime anywhere, but if caught drinking and driving abroad, foreigners have no rights and cannot be protected by American laws. They can lock people up and throw away the key, and there is nothing the American government can do about it, even if they wanted to. Don't drink and drive.

- Try to park as close as possible to the bar or nightclub. Have everyone take a mental note of the parking spot for later. Prevent parking in an area attractive to robbers by having the car parked by valet parking; this also gives your vehicle a better chance of being watched by security.
- Pay your own cover; don't become indebted to a nice stranger who offers to pay your way. Once you are inside, stay together as a group. Don't accept drinks, drugs, or anything else from strangers. If you decide to accept a drink, make sure you watch as it is being poured into the glass and served to you.
- *Be aware* and keep your guard up. Bars are public places and no one can predict or control who is going to walk through the door. Even private clubs, although somewhat better controlled, can still be a dangerous place.
- If an evening will be spent in a club or bar, don't carry a purse or wallet with a lot of cash or credit cards. Take only what you need for the night. Don't flaunt valuable items. This may cause unwanted attention, which in turn could entice someone to attempt a robbery. Keep valuables at home.
- Take it easy when drinking. Even though it may be tempting, try to pace drinking so focus and alertness can be maintained. Remember, you'll need to stay sober if you are the designated driver.

Tips for "Ladies' Night" on the Town

- Pay for your own drinks. Sometimes, when a man buys a woman a drink, he feels that he is entitled to spend

more time with the female, which makes him believe it will lead to other more intimate things.
- Don't send out the wrong signals. If someone is flirted with and led on and then all of a sudden cut off, this can make some guys mad, and some women, too. Don't lead someone on; let them know the rules up front.
- Keep an eye on your beverages. From the time the bartenders pours it until the time it is consumed, play close attention to the drink. Both women and men have had their drinks drugged while out partying. Men have been drugged and then taken somewhere by a woman with the intention of stealing his money and valuables before going on to the next victim in one of the hundreds of bars in her area. A woman can also be drugged, but with the objective by the man to have sex with her. This problem occurs more times than people would like to talk about it. So again, always keep an eye on your beverage.
- Have a bar purse that contains the least amount of valuables and ID-related material. Keep an eye on it, don't sit it down in the open, and only carry the minimum amount of money and credit cards needed. Running a tab is the easiest thing to do and in the long run, saves money since people are usually tipping on the whole night of drinks as opposed to every drink. This prevents digging through one's purse too often, thus resulting in less of a chance of something falling out. Remember, the less you carry, the less a thief can get.
- Keep drinking to a minimum. When people start to drink too much, they are more likely to be taken advantage of, and will not make the best decisions.
- Do not ever leave with someone upon first meeting them. Once in their vehicle, you are at a huge disadvantage. Control of your destination is now in the other person's hands, and if none of your family or friends knows your location, then the person driving can take advantage of you.

The key to staying safe in this situation is to have a plan before going out and sticking with it. Be aware of what is going on around the area, and ask yourself: Is it worth taking the chance? In some areas of the world, if you are honest with yourself, the answer is "No!"

On the Town and All Alone

So, all of the precautions have been taken, you have been careful, and have found someone that you've have met several times and would like to party with on the last night of vacation. How should the situation be handled safely? Remember, the person is still basically a stranger to you. Yes, he or she may be a nice person, but the objective is obvious: to go to either of your rooms. You will be alone with him or her, and this is where the problem lies. You still don't know what he or she is capable of doing once they get you alone.

Many women and men have gotten themselves in trouble by trusting someone they just met on vacation. The best way to deal with this is to not put yourself in this situation; that sounds like a real downer, but look at it this way: you get to choose between the known—going home without incident—and the unknown, which could be anything.

Women should pick five ways they can stay safe while they are traveling:

1.

2.

3.

4.

5.

Special Tips for Young Travelers

I have children, and I know there is nothing more important than their safety. With this being said, most parents do their children a disservice by trying to overprotect them. It is only normal that we try not to scare our children, but in doing so we are not teaching them to be aware of potential problems, or how to be "street smart." It is the duty of parents to teach them how to cope with situations in which they will have to make their own decisions. This is not easy for most parents, because they have to deal with their greatest fear: *something is happening to their child.*

What most parents don't understand is that children are much smarter than they are given credit for. Given the chance, kids can develop some great survival skills and make the right decisions at the right time. The problem is they don't know how to react to situations happening to them for the first time. No one does. In order for kids to make the right decisions, you must give the proper training and information along with having confidence in their ability to make the right choice. You can educate without scaring them. So, keep your kids informed.

- Have regular open discussions about personal security with them as much as possible.
- Even though it may seem difficult at times, review with your children their overall activities, and examine them to see how they can better keep themselves safe during their day-to-day activities.
- Explain to them (without making them overly paranoid) why limits are put on some of their activities, and why it so important to know who their friends are.

In order for a child to have an understanding of safety while on vacation, they must first have a basic understanding of day-to-day safety while they are at home.

Basic Things to Teach a Child Aged Four to Five Years Old

In case of an emergency, they should know their name, address, and phone number. Don't take it for granted that the children will just automatically know this information because you all live in the same house. Take the time to teach them, and then teach again to make sure they know this information inside and out.

Next, teach them not to give this information out to just anyone. At this age, let them know the difference between friends and strangers. Also make them aware that someone in a police or fire uniform can help them, and instruct your kids on dialing *911* in case of an emergency.

At this age, instruct your children to never give out information over the phone even when you're home with them. This will teach them at an early age, so that when they get older and are permitted to stay home for short periods of time, they will have the proper phone etiquette. *Under no conditions should children ever tell the caller that they are home alone.* The best advice for young children is to instruct them to only answer the phone when the parents call at a prearranged time, or if parents let the phone ring a certain number of times that only you and your child would know. To make things simpler, get caller ID.

Kids should be taught to never open the door for strangers, and to only let someone in whom parents have given permission to be let in. Teach them to avoid strangers and never accept rides from anyone they do not know. Make them understand that they must be told ahead of time that they were going to be picked up by the person they know.

I know this is an unpleasant thought, but you should prepare a plan of action in the event a child gets lost. You must have all of the pertinent information available, including a current picture of your child.

When children get older, parents will reluctantly have to give them some independence to do things and go places on their own. As a parent you will always worry, no matter how old they become, but understand that in order for them to grow into independent young adults, parents have to give them some freedom and at the same time give them the proper tools to see and deal with situations pertaining to their safety.

Safety Rules for Older Children

1. Always travel in groups or pairs.
2. Always walk along heavily traveled streets and avoid isolated areas.
3. Refuse automobile rides from strangers, and refuse to accompany strangers anywhere on foot.
4. Use city-approved play areas where adults supervise recreational activities.
5. Never leave home without telling their parents who they will be with and where they will be going.

During this time period, you should start to educate your child about his or her body, and what are considered the proper and improper places you can be touched by someone. Stress during this time how important it is to talk about *anything* that has happened that doesn't feel right.

To assure that a child has a grasp on these safety rules, work with them at their own pace until they have demonstrated an ability to follow this safety program.

The next two sections will help keep children safe while traveling on vacation.

In-room Safety

- Never leave young children in their room alone or unattended, and always be certain they are left in the hands of a responsible and trustworthy person.
- If the child is old enough and responsible to stay in the room for a short period of time, teach them proper in-room safety.

- Instruct children to *never* let anyone into the hotel room.
- When the parents leave the room, the kids should make sure the door is locked and chained.
- Instruct them to only leave the room in an emergency. Be sure to speak with them about fire safety, and what they should do in the event of an emergency.
- Make sure the child knows how to contact the front desk in case of an emergency, and they should always have a way to contact a parent.
- When answering a phone call while alone, they should never let anyone know they are alone. If the caller asks for a parent, the child should explain that the parent is busy or in the shower and ask to take a message.
- Parents should leave the "Do Not Disturb" sign on the door when exiting.

City Smarts

- The number one thing to always stress to children is to never talk to strangers or accept gifts or rides. If someone tries to bother or grab them, they should run away screaming, and if they have to, fight back.
- Leave the expensive shoes and jackets at home. These types of items may draw unwanted attention to a child and can possibly get him or her set up for a robbery.
- Make sure children know their full names, address, city, state, and phone number with area code, plus both of their parents' first and last names. If the kids get separated from their parents, they should know the names of the hotel where they are staying. Make sure that they know not to reveal this information to anyone except a police officer, doctor, or nurse.
- When out sightseeing or at an amusement park, agree on a rendezvous place in the event anyone gets separated. Most people can keep in contact by cell phone.

- If one of the children does become lost, teach them to seek help from a police officer in uniform or someone who works in the place they are lost.
- Always escort a child to the restroom. Never assume children are safe.
- Establish a family code word. Teach a child to never go with anyone who doesn't know the secret code word.
- Don't flash money out in public. Someone is always watching.

In order for a child to be able to react in case of emergency parents must practice with them verbally, and then through role-playing. This is why parents should have a child train in the martial arts. Besides giving them the obvious benefits like fitness, confidence, and better focus, it will also teach them to stay cool and calm under pressure and have a better chance of successfully dealing with a safety crisis.

List five ways you can keep your children safe while on vacation:

1.

2.

3.

4.

5.

Traveling in the "Golden Years"

Unfortunately, senior citizens have become a neglected group in our society over the last couple of decades. It is our duty and responsibility to make their "golden years" both safe and happy, but this is sometimes more easily said than done. Many senior citizens are still healthy and active and want to stay independent. They also have more discretionary spending and enjoy traveling.

Keeping these attributes is important to everyone, but it works to a criminal's advantage to find an older person who is alone. When it comes to choosing a potential victim to commit a crime against, senior citizens are at the top of the list. While traveling and vacationing, senior citizens have to look out for crimes like scams, push-in robbers, muggings and purse snatchings, and carjackings. Compared to the past, there are now more criminals, therefore more crimes are being committed.

Criminals have also become more violent. This is especially important for senior citizens to know, because a criminal is more likely to hurt them during a crime if they don't cooperate. This is why it is so important to have the knowledge to deal with this, if and when confronted.

Special Tips for Senior Travelers

Don't trust strangers. Don't vacation alone. This means travel with other people or vacation where there will be plenty of other people around all the time. By doing so, seniors can look out for each other. When senior citizens are by themselves, unscrupulous people will try and take advantage of their perceived weakness. Most people are very respectful of senior citizens, but criminals see senior citizens as easy targets.

Watch out for "push-ins." There are two ways this crime can be committed. The first way is when a criminal lurks behind someone while they unlock their door. Right when the victim is about to enter their room, the criminal pushes the victim inside and they are at their mercy. The second way is when someone is already in his or her room and a stranger knocks on the door pretending to be an employee of the hotel. If the victim opens the door, the intruder will push their way in. In both cases, the best defense is to be aware of the problem and stay alert, and to never open the door for any strangers.

On vacation, plan ahead of time not to buy anything unless it is from a legitimate store or shop. When purchasing, try to pay by credit card or traveler's check.

Don't fall for con artists, con games, or scams. These are the most notorious crimes against senior citizens besides consumer fraud. While on vacation, there will be many opportunities for tourists to spend money. Depending on the location, there will be merchants with carts on the streets, kids running up trying to sell something, or little shops lined up ready to sell to the foreigners who come every day with lots of cash.

The problem with many of these merchants is they like to use pressure tactics to get people to buy their merchandise. If one is not used to these types of tactics, they can be very intimidating. As senior citizens, some unscrupulous merchants will try to take advantage of you because of your age, feeling that there is nothing seniors can do about it. In order to successfully deal with this, discuss it with whomever you are traveling and set limits on how much you are willing to spend. Know how to walk away and not get caught up in any type of bartering.

There are so many types of scams and cons out there that volumes of books could be written on the subject. Remember the golden rule: "If it sounds too good to be true, it is." Simple games on the street like "Three Card Molly," the sale of fake Rolex watches, or the many types of scams where the victim has to take money out of the bank worked twenty-five years ago, and some versions of them are still working now. The reason they will always work is because it is human nature to want something for nothing.

The people who run these scams know this better than anyone else. They are experts on how to play to the greed factor. It's pretty hard for the average middle-class person to keep up with a quick-witted streetwise person whose job is to relieve you of your money and does this every day. Unfortunately, these same characters love nothing better than to take advantage of the unsuspecting senior citizens who comes to the area on vacation. The best way to not fall prey to these types of crimes is not to buy into the dream and get caught up in it. Don't fall for anything that sounds too good to be true. Walk away.

Traveling by Car

Many senior citizens vacation by car and enjoy the more relaxed stop-and-go, keeping control of where they go, and having a "how long I can stay" attitude. If this is the way you like to travel and are physically able to, you should do it. Your goal is to enjoy yourself while on vacation—but your safety should always be on your mind.

- Don't get complacent while driving.
- Keep your doors locked when in the vehicle.
- Always keep the windows up, and keep the vehicle in gear when in slow or stopped traffic.
- Always keep space between your vehicle and the vehicle in front of you at a stoplight or when traffic has slowed down; this is to give enough room to drive off in case of an attempted carjacking.
- Never let the fuel fall below a quarter of a tank.
- Never pick up hitchhikers.
- Don't keep any valuables out in the open where they can be seen.
- Don't leave the keys in the car.
- Keep a charged cell phone on you at all times. Always stay in touch with someone so your location is always known.

For more tips on staying safe while driving, see chapter Four: Car Safety on the Road

For tips on how to stay safe while in your hotel, see chapter Seven: Hotel and Motel Safety

For tips on how to stay safe while out on the streets, see chapter Thirteen: Staying "Street Smart" in Unfamiliar Cities

Chapter Fifteen

Personal Safety and Self-defense

Self-defense Training: You Don't Have to Be a Black Belt to Defend Yourself

This entire book is about self-defense. Avoidance and prevention is 90 percent of self-defense. If a person can see and understand a situation before it happens, they will have options and a better chance of responding to or defusing an attack. However, even when all the proper precautions are taken and everything is done correctly, this may still not be enough. One may be put into a situation where there is no choice but to face it head on. Once the situation has escalated, and there is a chance that it may become physical, do you have the tools to successfully deal with it? No matter who you are, you can only be successful during a confrontation or physical attack if you have had some form of training in self-defense.

The choice is yours: *How will you deal with a situation when it comes to your safety?*

You can:

- Ignore the facts and go through everyday life thinking that it could never happen.
- Live in complete fear and spend time worrying about becoming a victim of crime.
- Prepare yourself for the possibility of becoming a victim by getting self-defense training along with awareness training, which will provide anyone with a better chance of dealing with a potential attack.

Taking a Self-defense Class

When choosing a self-defense class, your most important question is: are the instructors really training for self-defense, or for tournament fighting? Granted, any class that stresses physical conditioning and combat training is a good start for giving someone confidence and preparation. But if the training stresses rules, they are barking up the wrong tree. All martial arts—karate, kickboxing, jujitsu, grappling, and boxing—are tough sports, but in order to make them street effective, one must include dirty fighting. The ideal situation would be to have a mixture of all of these disciplines. This way the student will have the ability to deal with any type of fighting style that they may encounter on the street. This is where a good instructor comes in. Do your homework before joining a self-defense class.

Picking the Right Instructor for You

If self-defense is the goal, when looking for an instructor the prospective student should look past all the trophies in the windows or how high the instructor can kick. Research his or her qualifications and experience. Does one have to be a black belt before they can defend themselves, or are the techniques taught easy to learn and effective? Here are some things to find out about an instructor *before* joining his or her class.

- How long have they been teaching?
- What are their credentials as an instructor?
- Does he or she have a good "bedside" manner?
- Is there open class viewing?
- Does training include nonverbal *and* verbal self-defense? (Most martial arts schools don't train their students in this second area.)
- Does the instructor stress safety in class?
- Is the instructor training for realistic self-defense?
- Does the instructor practice role-playing and scenario training?

The Importance of a Positive Mind-set

The key to successfully protecting yourself and feeling confident enough to fight back begins in the mind. You must feel enough self-value to fight for yourself. There is no single correct way to react to a confrontation. Any choice of action taken while under attack is the right choice at that time, but if you want to make the choice of defending yourself and coming out on top, then first prepare yourself mentally. Develop options that fit your personality.

In order to feel confident about fighting back when defending against an attacker, preparation is a *must*. If faced with an attack, think positively and believe that you have the skills necessary to deal with it. With each self-defense situation, one will need to have options. Should you fight back, submit, run, etc.? The only way to successfully pick the right decision at that particular time is to practice different scenarios with different options ahead of time. By using strategies and practicing defending against various attacks in a variety of situations, you will have more confidence in defending yourself. Whether you are training or an actual situation is about to take place, one must believe in themselves 110 percent. Train for realistic self-defense by sharpening up the weapons of your body and by conditioning and focusing on the basic skills and attributes of unarmed and armed self-defense. By perfecting these skills, you will have given yourself the confidence needed to come out on top when confronted.

Visualization Skills

One of the skills that will help enhance and improve self-defense training is visualization. Visualization is the process of creating pictures or images in the mind. Whereas language is thinking with words, visualization is thinking with pictures. It is using your imagination to see with the "mind's eye." When recreating images in the mind, one must also create feelings, sensations, and emotions to accompany these images. Mental visualization is an effective way to improve techniques, maneuvers against an attack, and strategic assessment.

This valuable skill can be used in many ways to improve ourselves, but here we will focus on its use in preparing self-defense. For visualization to work at its best, one must first achieve a deep state of calmness and relaxation, free from distractions.

Here's a basic example of how to attain a state of relaxation:

- Sit in a chair with your back straight, arms relaxed and uncrossed, with both feet on the floor; or lie down on something comfortable with arms to the side, legs straight out.
- First, close your eyes, relax the body and focus on clearing the mind of all outside thoughts, focusing only on the moment.
- Next, take deep, slow breaths and stay relaxed, keeping the mind clear.
- Once the mind is relaxed and breathing is under control, do the following exercise to ensure the relaxation of the body. Tense every muscle in the body at once. Start out by tensing up the toes, feet, legs, buttocks, chest, shoulders, arms, and fists, then, tighten your jaw and

facial muscles. Hold the tension for about ten to fifteen seconds, and then let go, allowing the tension to flow out of the body.

The next exercise concerns the *actual confrontation.* There are literally thousands of situations you can encounter when dealing with safety. I will give a simple example of how to use visualization skills to be better prepared in the event a self-defense situation arises.

Visualize walking out to your car in a parking lot at night. You are doing all the right things, scanning the immediate area, walking in the middle of the parking row. Suddenly, an uneasy feeling is in your stomach. As your heart rate speeds up, you control it along with your breathing to keep a handle on things. You recall the training you have had. You are nervous but confident. You are prepared for anything that comes your way. As you start to perspire, you can really feel the cool wind blow against your face.

Out of the shadows comes a short but stocky man who walks up and then stops about ten feet from you. You are nervous, but you stay in control. He looks at you, and you are returning eye contact. In your mind you tell him, "It's your move."

This simple return of eye contact tells the stranger that you are not easily intimidated. Your heart is racing at two hundred miles per hour, but you begin to control it.

All of a sudden, the stranger asks for a couple of dollars. You take a deep breath and reply, "Don't have it, sorry." You say this slowly and in control, not giving any suggestion that you are afraid or scared. Your body language is giving off positive self-confidence. You both stand there another ten seconds, and then the stranger turns around to walk away.

As you watch him walk away, you scan the area one more time to make sure there is no one else around. Then walk to your car, checking under and inside of it first. As you get in and lock the door, you still know this is not the time to relax. You drive away, still focused on your surroundings, only relaxing once you get home and in your house.

You may have to run through this situation several times in your mind in order to make it clear and realistic. This is just one example. Other examples of this same situation follow:

- Someone unexpectedly runs up and attempts a robbery
- There is more than one person
- A weapon is not involved
- A weapon is involved
- Gun, knife, club, etc.
- Do they threaten or do they just attack?
- Did you see him coming, or did he catch you off guard?
- Is there any dialogue?

Listed below are a few questions which should be asked when visualizing different scenarios.

- Do I have any self-defense training?
- Do I have the skills to verbally defuse a potentially dangerous situation?
- Can I run away or am I trapped?
- Do I know the person?
- Does the person seem fearful or angry?
- Is the person intoxicated or on drugs?

Now, take that same situation we talked about earlier and see how many ways it can change. As an attack is visualized, see yourself assuming a stance, vividly striking your attacker or attackers with kicks and punches and strikes to vulnerable points on the human body. During the attack one must feel the strikes, and hear the breaking of bones, on the attacker's body. Listen to the attacker grunt in pain and scream in agony. In order for visualization to work, deal with the same situation in at least four different ways. Experiment with different combative scenarios, changing the circumstance, environment, opponent, and range. When deciding to defend against an attacker, do so 100 percent. When defending yourself, you must give everything you have in retaliation, and expect to come out on top.

Awareness Skills

Knowledge and awareness of one's surroundings are critical ingredients of any self-defense plan. It's impossible to stay on high alert all the time. It can burn you out and make you paranoid. A good example of appropriate awareness is this: when you're at home, you can let your guard down and relax, but when on the streets, you must be on alert. Always be aware of what is going on around you, but don't be on high alert all of the time. The best way to handle this is to understand the different types of criminals.

Regardless of what people think or have heard, bad guys are not all stupid or dumb. The smart ones understand human behavior and are capable of assessing body language, the way people walk and talk, and if someone is afraid. Above all, they know how to exploit these weaknesses. So the best thing for you is to know how criminals think and what they are looking for. For example, if a criminal is out to steal from someone, they have certain tactics they will use to take victims by surprise. The attacker may or may not have a weapon while they are committing the act, but sometimes the element of surprise is more dangerous than the actual weapon. When caught off guard, it is much harder to regroup.

There are different degrees of awareness when it comes to personal safety. A color code warning system originated by the military for the U.S. Marines during World War II follows:

Condition White: The remote possibility of danger is not perceived. The individual is unprepared and relaxed.

Condition Yellow: Relaxed awareness of the immediate environment which, though seemingly benign, does have some element of potential danger.

Condition Orange: A potential unknown danger transpires. React accordingly.

Code Red: An actual violent situation with a dangerous opponent transpires.

Code Black: An extreme situation is in progress, and a fight for one's life is a reality.

Many self-defense experts use this color code system or a variation of it for civilian use. This system will give everyday citizens a measuring tool for awareness and how to gauge it.

What the Average Criminal Looks for Before Attacking

- When and where to attack
- The time potential targets will least expect an attack
- Potential targets who are alone
- Darkness
- A deserted area
- Potential victims who are unaware of the environment
- An individual who looks like a "victim"

How do they Attack?

- From behind, very close or in contact
- From the side, very close or in contact
- Directly in front, about eight feet away
- Directly in front, very close or in contact
- Charging from any direction

This is why it is necessary to stay alert and be aware. By seeing what is happening ahead of time, this will give you more options and more time to deal with the situation.

Criminal Awareness

The next skill is *criminal awareness*. It involves an understanding and knowledge of a criminal's motivations and what makes him tick. Keep yourself informed of global incidents through the media, official crime reports, and other sources. By doing this, knowledge is gained of the types and trends of violent acts and their reasons behind it.

When speaking on criminal awareness, the subject is so vast that it is best to stick with the basics. As you study this subject, personalities of various violent aggressors will become more familiar. Study their mannerisms and any other information available. By opening your mind, eyes, and ears, your assessment skills and incumbent understanding will be enhanced, and the risk of victimization will begin to diminish.

Situational Awareness

Situational awareness is the element of total alertness, presence, and focus on everything in your immediate surroundings. Train your senses to detect and assess the people, places, objects, and actions that may pose a danger. When situational awareness skills are developed, signals of confidence, awareness, and strength are sent out. Anyone who is paying attention will see a very assertive and purposeful person. To a criminal, this person will not be an easy target.

Situational awareness will also diminish a criminal's favorite weapon: the element of surprise. With the ability to see and detect danger, it will be harder for a criminal or thug to set you up for a multitude of crimes, because you know what to expect and how to respond.

Develop all five of your senses to help develop your situation awareness skills, along with the powers of instinct and intuition. By having the ability to detect problems before they happen, anyone can avoid a potential problem.

Self-awareness

People ask themselves, "What does being self-aware have to do with self-defense?" *Self-awareness* has plenty to do with self-defense! In order for anyone to be able to realistically protect themselves, they must know both their strengths and weaknesses, and then be open-minded enough to make some changes.

Physical strengths and weaknesses. It is critical to know your physical strengths and weaknesses. The physical condition you are in or how skilled you are defending yourself will dictate how you will deal with confrontation. If you are out of shape, overweight, or small framed, will your body language and the manner in which you carry yourself most likely deter or provoke an attack? Do you have any type of training in self-defense? If not, could you run fast enough and far enough to successfully get away from a potential attacker? Could you defend yourself against a knife or a gun? Or do you feel that, if attacked, there is nothing you could do about it and you would be at the attacker's mercy? These are not easy questions to answer, but by honestly doing so, this will help you figure out what you need to practice and learn to successfully fend off crime.

Mental attributes. Mental strengths and weakness are a main factor for self-defense and coming out on top. Can you handle stress, and when doing so will you be able to stay strong and confident, and step up to the plate when dealing with your safety? Everyone has fears, but if you cannot control yourself and panic easily under pressure, you're putting yourself at a great disadvantage. You must be "mentally tough" in order to cope.

Communications skills. How well can you express yourself while under pressure? Do you lose focus or get rattled if someone verbally attacks you? Do you have the skills to defuse a potentially hostile situation and feel comfortable about it? The old adage, "Those are fighting words," means that things have gone too far. Words will not help solve the problem. This is why having the ability to communicate adequately under stressful situations is so important. This skill alone can prevent a fight.

Personality. What type of person do you think you are? Are you open—or closed-minded? Are you aggressive or passive? Are you laid back, or are you loud and a pain in the butt? By answering these kinds of questions, you will have a better understanding as to how you will react under pressure, and what you need to perfect in order to be at your best in the event of a potentially violent situation.

Age and gender. The crime of which people are most likely to become a victim has a lot to do with their sex and age. An elderly person will fall victim to certain crimes (purse snatchings, scams, home invasions) because of their age and not being able to physically defend themselves, as well as very young children. Women will more likely become a victim of robbery or rape, while youth are more likely to be molested or kidnapped. Understanding this information will help you and your loved ones take better care of yourselves, and most importantly not become victims.

Assessment skills. The ability to successfully assess a dangerous situation quickly and accurately can sometimes be the difference between life and death. In the event you have to assess a potentially dangerous situation, you need to have a clear and level head and have great observational skills. In order to make the right decision, you have to make quick and rapid assessments and *trust* your decision. Gather information about the immediate environment, the threatening individual, and yourself.

The environment. If a dangerous situation arises, quickly take notice of the surroundings. If an escape is necessary, you should have a plan to do so as soon as possible. Here are some things to consider when making this important decision.

- Where are all possible routes of escape?
- How many people are in proximity, and are they friend or foe?
- What types of objects are around that can serve as barriers?
- Are there any objects that can be used as a weapon or a shield?
- Are there any other people around who can hear or see what is going on?

The Threatening Individual. Criminals come in all shapes and sizes. Don't ever judge someone by the way they look. When you assess a person, read their body language and how they carry themselves. Are they aggressive, or cool and calm? Look for anything that will tell you that a person is about to attack.

- Do you know who this person is, and what do you know about them?

- How close is this person, and are they blocking the escape?
- How big and strong are they?
- What is this person's state of mind?
- What are they saying and how is it being said?
- Do they possess a weapon or is there anything to use as a weapon?

You. In order to successfully handle a violent situation, you the individual must realistically assess who you are and what you are capable of doing. Here are a few things to answer to get a more accurate assessment of yourself.

- What *skills* do you possess that will help you deal with this type of situation?
- What are your *strengths*?
- Do you feel *confident* enough to deal with attempted crimes?

De-escalation. De-escalation techniques consist of verbal, psychological, and nonverbal techniques for defusing potentially dangerous situations. These techniques are an important part of self-defense training and are an effective way to postpone a physical attack. In order for de-escalation techniques to work, the defender must stay in control of his or her feelings in order to build a rapport and a sense of connectedness with an agitated person. By using this technique in the first stage of confrontation, you can reduce the likelihood of an escalation into physical violence. There are both verbal and nonverbal principles involved in de-escalating a situation.

Nonverbal De-escalation Skills

I'm sure everyone has heard the old saying, "It's not always what you say, but how you say it." Nonverbal behavior accounts for 70 percent of communication. Pitch, inflection, and volume account for 25 percent while less than 7 percent has to do with the choice of words. Here are the skills you'll want to perfect in order to show confidence when using de-escalation techniques.

Project a Confident and Calm Manner:

- Maintain eye contact.
- Have a relaxed face and an alert posture.
- Keep hand and body movements to a minimum.
- Control the breathing, doing so deeply and slowly from the diaphragm and not the chest.
- Keep positive thoughts about the situation and how to handle it.

Positioning Yourself for Safety:

- Try to keep at least ten feet away from a potential assailant.
- Keep your body at a forty-five-degree angle to present fewer targets if you have to defend yourself.
- Keep hands free and in front of the body.
- If something is available, move behind it.

Verbal De-escalation Skills

- When speaking with a potential attacker, do so in a calm and steady voice, while speaking slowly and evenly.
- Actively listen to what the person is saying.
- If the person is upset, acknowledge his or her feelings.
- Communicate clearly your intentions and your expectations.
- Try to avoid any escalating behaviors.

In order to properly use these different strategies and techniques in a real situation, practice different scenarios and participate in role-playing in order to feel comfortable and be able to perform them under stress.

Fighting skills. How much do you value yourself? Do you feel that you are worth fighting for? In order to fight back effectively, you must first believe you are worth defending. If you decide to fight back, it must be a personal choice. The main thing to remember is that whatever choice you decide on is the right choice at the time. Unfortunately, whether you choose to resist, submit, or negotiate, there is no guarantee that fighting back will thwart every attack.

Practice and self-defense training builds the confidence you will require in your personal skills. Confidence comes from being prepared. As you train with confidence and intensity, you will increase your chances of protecting yourself successfully.

The natural weapons of your body must be trained. Each attack is different, so you'll need to be able to respond in a variety of ways. When deciding to fight back, see and believe you will win every encounter you are faced with. Pick your targets and strike back with full conviction. Feelings of fear must be dealt with. This is nature. Use it to your advantage, like a shot of turbo energy. You must have breath control, stay focused, and do whatever is necessary to survive.

The first thing you focus on in self-defense training is *defense*. An ineffective punch or kick is easy to execute. However, it is not normal to have people throw punches at you; it's much harder to block a strike properly. If you are not trained to handle an attack, you will tense up and freeze when someone throws a strike. The sooner your defense is perfected, the more confident your skills will become.

Defense

Personal self-defense stance. This must be a stance that allows you to move in and out from the attacker quickly and still protect yourself. Here are some rules for forming an effective stance:

- The body must be positioned at a forty-five-degree angle, so as to not expose vital organs to an attack and to have better balance.
- Keep the hands in front of the body, relaxed and ready to block or strike.
- Keeping the body relaxed and control your breathing.

- You must maintain distance between yourself and an attacker at all times.
- When in the stance of your choice, convey confidence.

With a minimum amount of training, footwork can be used to stay out of harm's way.

Two neutralizing techniques follow that can be used to render an opponent's attack ineffective:

Evasion—Moves that involve shielding the body from the line of attack, i.e., running away, sidestepping, or ducking.

Sidestepping—A move that can be used to evade an attacker who is attacking head on. After using this move, either run away or strike back.

After learning how to evade an attack, learn how to *block*. A block is when the arm is used to stop or redirect an attack from an attacker. If someone throws a punch or kick, redirect it from striking the different areas that are more serious, like the face, throat, or groin. There are two types of blocks to use. The block used will depend on what position the attacker is facing. One, the *inward block*, which is a right-arm block, used to redirect a right-hand strike away from the center line. Two, the *outward block*, again a right-arm block, to sweep a right-hand strike away from the center line.

Parries—the principle of blocking is the same, but with the use of open palms of the hand.

If someone throws a kick, the principles of blocking are the same, only lower. The feet can also be used to stop an oncoming kick.

Yelling in self-defense. Yelling, or what they call in the martial arts the *"kia,"* is a very powerful weapon. It is used to startle, distract, and temporarily paralyze the opponent. By doing the *kia*, an opponent is sometimes frozen in his tracks, which will allow that split-second advantage needed to gain control over the attacker. He may also think you are crazy and suspend the attack.

Counterstrikes. You can't just keep blocking strikes all day. Sooner or later one of the blows will make contact. This is why counterstrikes are effective, after blocking an incoming blow.

In order for a strike to be effective, it must be delivered to vulnerable targets on the human body. When trained properly, you should be able to deliver strikes that cause pain, including major injury.

Vulnerable targets of the human body. If your life or the life of your loved ones is on the line, you have to be ready to do what it takes to protect yourself and them. Don't be squeamish about hurting someone. The key to making counterstrikes work is to keep striking at the vulnerable targets on an attacker's body until he goes down, or it is safe to run away. The most vulnerable targets on the human body are *eyes, throat, groin,* and *knees.*

Striking any one of these targets in an attack can stop even the largest and angriest person, if done properly. Only strike these areas if it is a life-or-death situation.

Secondary targets on the human body. A blow to any one of these targets, when done properly, can cause great injury and pain.

Front Upper Body

- temples
- nose
- jaw
- chin
- side of neck

Front Middle Body

- solar plexus
- floating ribs
- upper abdomen
- lower abdomen

Front Lower Body

- thighs
- knees
- shins
- insteps

Rear Upper Body

- base of neck
- spine
- kidneys

Rear Lower Body

- back of legs
- side of knees

Weapons of the Body

Hand Strikes

- jab
- cross
- eye gouge
- palm heel strike
- web hand strike
- hammer fist

Kicks

- front kick
- side kick
- round kick
- back kick
- stomp kick

Close Range

- elbows
- knees
- head butt
- biting
- thumb and finger gouge

Grappling

Jujitsu and other grappling arts have become very popular over the past decade and are valuable skills to learn. Even though you may not have the time to perfect this art, you should learn the basics in your self-defense program. Another reason to incorporate grappling is to gain knowledge to defend against someone who uses grappling in a self-defense situation. In a real life or death situation, avoid going to the ground to grapple. The attacker may have some friends just waiting to jump in and try to smash your head into the ground. Use close quarter techniques to neutralize your attacker. The use of head butts, biting, clawing, and gouging techniques must be used in order to offset an assailant who is trying to crowd or throw you down. The key thing to remember is: *Never grapple with a grappler; never box with a boxer.* Keep everything to your advantage.

Weapons—Pros and Cons

Since we are talking about safety pertaining to traveling, when speaking of weapons we will take into consideration the restraints and the strict laws that come with carrying weapons while traveling abroad.

Lethal Weapons

Guns. Besides the obvious reasons for not carrying a gun while traveling, if you do have a gun in the home or carry one legally, you must be trained to handle a firearm. Also realize that once a gun is used, it is final. People die. If you are not willing to use deadly force, and you hesitate, the gun can be taken and used against you.

While traveling in the U.S.A., if you have a permit, it is legal to carry a gun in certain states. When traveling by plane, the airline will make a record of the weapon and will store it in checked luggage until your destination is reached. Before even considering taking a gun on your travels, make sure it is legal to carry one in the state you are visiting. Unless someone is in the security business and a firearm is needed in that line of work, it is not worth trying to travel with a firearm when flying. If traveling by other forms of transportation, it is easier to carry a gun. But remember, make sure it is legal and you have a permit before traveling to another city or state. *When traveling abroad, don't even think about bringing a weapon on your trip.*

If you are thinking about buying a gun from someone once you have reached your destination, forget about it. Remember, if you are caught with a firearm in most countries, they will give you a stiff sentence, have you thrown in prison, and there is *nothing* the U.S.A. can do.

Knives. A knife can be concealed very easily on the human body. If traveling by plane, simply pack the knife in your luggage. Just like a gun, a knife in the hands of a beginner can be dangerous, but in the hands of an expert can be deadly. Having trained many police and law enforcement officers over the years, the majority of them say that they fear a knife more than a gun at close quarter combat. Just like a gun, don't pull it out unless you are willing to use it. Hesitate for just a second, and someone can take it away and use it against you.

Nonlethal Weapons

Pepper spray and Mace. Pepper spray, which is made from the extracts of peppers, has replaced Mace, a chemical spray. Pepper spray is meant to be a deterrent to crime. In order to be effective, it must be out and ready to use. If it's in your purse or inside your pocket, the spray will do no good in the event of an emergency. The other problem with this type of weapon is, if the wind is blowing in your direction, you can very easily spray yourself by accident. It also doesn't affect all attackers the same way, and the attacker could take it and spray you in the face. Always practice with your pepper spray.

Stun gun. It looks vicious—when pushing the trigger, a flashing blue arc of electricity and a popping sound will be a visual deterrent to most people. The attacker must be within arm's reach for it to work. This could be too close for most people. It can also take several seconds of contact to immobilize an assailant. With the stress of an attack, it will be hard to touch a person if he or she starts to fight back.

Personal Alarms. These are designed to draw attention to the situation. There is no guarantee that just because people hear it, they will come to the rescue. If you must use one, do so as a distraction, and then run away.

Commonly Carried Everyday Weapons

Everyday items that people often carry can be used as effective self-defense weapons. If your intention is to use these items as self-defense weapons in an emergency, first prepare yourself both mentally and physically to do so. Have the knowledge and ability to know when to use the weapons of choice and how to use them. Defensive actions must be swift and forceful. The number one rule here is: you *must* use the element of surprise.

Here are the items that can be improvised and used as weapons:

- book
- comb
- pen or pencil

- fork
- umbrella
- walking cane
- belt
- keys
- nail file
- briefcase
- cell phone

Defending Against Weapons

There is always a chance you will have to defend against a weapon. If a man takes out a knife or club, you should usually run away, but if there is a gun involved, it has to be handled differently. How someone does this depends on how they have trained. There are no absolutes when protecting yourself, but you want to greatly reduce the odds that you will freeze up due to lack of experience. And the reality is, empty-hand self-defense has to be learned first *before* training against weapons. You need a solid foundation in order to survive a weapon attack.

Ten Commandments of Self-defense

1. *Fight Dirty.* Never use bare hands when there is something around that can be picked up to hit your attacker with. If escaping the situation isn't possible, then fight with all your might and never give up. Again, if there is something around to use as a weapon, use it! Since there are no rules in a real fight, and your life is on the line, do whatever it takes to win and come out alive.
2. *Attack the Vital Areas.* When in a serious encounter, don't waste time or energy throwing sparring techniques at your attacker. You should focus on attacking the four main targets of self-defense: eyes, throat, groin, and knees. When protecting yourself against dangerous criminals, keep your attack simple and to the point. Above all, do not attempt anything fancy.

3. *Don't Be Defensive: Attack the Attacker.* Against a real attack, use the strategy of surprise with a quick and powerful attack. A rational individual never seeks or condones violence as a way of dealing with people, but if someone confronts you with the intentions of doing bodily harm, then turn the tables on them and strike first and fast. Attack the attacker first. This is not the time to be defensive. The sooner you attack, the sooner you will insure your own safety.
4. *Keep your Techniques Simple and Easy.* Do not confuse fighting techniques that look pretty with what works. The best techniques are the ones that are simple and direct. Being able to kick someone in the head is impressive, but this doesn't guarantee the technique will be effective in a real attack. Low kicks, elbow and knee strikes, short hand strikes, head butting, and even biting, spitting, and gouging constitute what is reliable, although unpleasant.
5. *Never Attempt to Threaten or Bluff; Never "Warn" an Attacker.* These are ploys used by inexperienced combatants. Any experienced street fighter or criminal will read right through this ploy and realize that this person is not confident in what he is doing. There are some de-escalation techniques that can be used in the beginning of some confrontations, but once it reaches the next stage all the talking in the world will not help. Don't announce that you will kill him if he takes another step, or tell him that you are a "killing machine." Once you have reached this point, there is no talking, bluffing, threatening, or warning. Never warn anyone that you are capable of resistance. This will not scare the attacker. All it will do is prepare the assailant to be more vicious in his attack. Those are the facts, so be ready to defend yourself to whatever extent possible.
6. *Expect to Get Hurt.* No matter how good someone is, what style of fighting he or she has been taught, or how tough they are convinced their training has made them, they should expect to absorb some punishment. Here is a fact of life: *troublemakers, bullies, and violent criminals of all types are not pushovers.* They may not be trained in a particular

fighting style, but they are experienced in violence and have been hurt and have hurt people before. They just chalk it up as a part of doing business. *So if someone attacks with a knife, how does one respond?*

As we discussed, you prepare for such an attack mentally. This comes through knowledge and practice. Remember our rule: if running away is not an option, if there is something to pick up and use as a weapon, *use it*. If you have no choice but to defend yourself empty-handed, being mentally prepared to deal with the situation and come out on top helps a great deal. No one wants to get cut or stabbed, but if one's life is on the line, a knife-wielding maniac has to be dealt with. Defend yourself, and expect to be cut. Minimize any dangerous cuts, taking them on the outer arms and legs. Avoid any cut or stab to the throat, chest, stomach, and the inner arms and legs. The key here again is to maintain a mind-set to deal with any situation that may come your way. *Remember, pain is only temporary . . . death is forever.*

7. *Keep in shape.* Physical conditioning is an important part of self-defense. I'm not saying to be in shape like a professional boxer, or a college wrestler, but the better shape you're in, the more confidence you will have. The degree of physical strength, speed, agility, and stamina dictates at least 50 percent of your fighting skills in the street. Besides self-defense training, include some strength training, cardiovascular training, and stretching. The more you take care of your body, the better your body can take care of you in times of crisis.

8. *Stay alert at all times.* Staying alert and being aware is the first lesson in personal safety and self-defense. Be constantly aware of your surroundings and anyone acting suspiciously out in public. Being "street smart" begins with an awareness of others and having the experience to read their intentions through their body language, and then acting accordingly. Don't get lackadaisical when you are out in public. Stay focused and alert at all times.

9. *Avoid going to the ground with an attacker.* In the past few years, jujitsu and grappling have become very popular because of the NHB (No Holds Barred) fighting. Having grappling

skills can only be a plus in a street fight. With this being said, in a real confrontation you should stay on your feet if at all possible. If you go to the ground with someone in a fight, don't be surprised to be met with the feet of some of his friends going upside your head and face. The only good thing about this is if you learn how to grapple, there is a better chance of defending against it, which makes it harder for someone to take you down.

10. *Prepare your mind and body mentally.* I know it's been mentioned plenty of times, but the first part of your preparation must be to have a plan. It would be nice if we could go through life without a care in the world, but unfortunately life isn't like that. No matter how careful we are about things, something will go wrong when we least expect it. One can be alert and minimize the chances of becoming a victim, but if focus and awareness is lost, then anyone can be caught off guard and become a victim of crime. You should know what you are going to do before an attack and prepare for it ahead of time. *Have a plan.* It will give you the confidence to come out a winner.

Conclusion

No matter where we are or what we are doing, our safety should subconsciously be a full-time job. *Be prepared.* But remember, you only get out of it what you put in. If you only learn the awareness skills and not the physical, and are in a situation where you may need to defend yourself, you will hesitate, because you didn't prepare yourself for an attack.

Why take the chance of becoming a crime victim? Make an investment in yourself and loved ones so if you have to deal with an attack, you will have the physical tools and, most importantly, the mental toughness to deal with violence.

Believe it or not, physical self-defense is the last line of defense. While it is true that some conflicts cannot be de-escalated once they have reached a certain level, it is also true that a majority of attacks can be avoided before they reach a physical level of violence. In order to successfully face any type of attack or crime, first know something about the enemy and have a plan on how to respond. Develop a personal self-defense strategy.

Create a high sense of awareness in order to be savvy enough to recognize something is about to happen. Make the proper decisions to address any issue. Since self-defense is 90 percent awareness, it would behoove you to develop observation skills, and if a situation seems threatening, choose the right strategy that will allow you to escape unharmed. If cornered and all other forms of escape have failed, have the ability to click into *autopilot,* pick the right strategy for that particular situation, and use it for protection. This can only be done by training and practice.

This book was written to educate the public on how to remain safe while traveling. It doesn't stop there. Like anything else that is important, it must become a way of life. The safety of you and your family is and should be a full-time job. Training for safety is not something that should be a burden, but more like insurance.

If you apply the information in this book and put it to use, be assured, it will someday help you in a time of need. No amount of money can replace the satisfaction of knowing that that you were able to do something that kept you and your loved ones safe.

Synopsis

How to Vacation and Travel Safely . . . and Come Back Alive begins with the real-life story of how author Earnest Hart Jr. was held captive in Thailand while visiting for a series of kickboxing matches. Hart felt vulnerable in this foreign land where the government was run by a military that imposed their will upon the foreign contestants with Uzis and intimidation.

Forced to realize that the world we live in is as dangerous outside of the ring as it is inside, Hart continued his martial arts training and added to his knowledge by studying all available material related to security.

. . . I didn't get a bit of sleep that night. I sat up in my bed with my back to the wall, looking at the door and hoping no one would come through it. I started to wonder if I was ever going to get back to the U. S. alive. No one outside of Thailand really knew where I was. The most important questions I went over many times during that night were, "How could I have prevented this from happening, and how do I get out of this situation?"

Since 9/11, personal safety has never been more paramount. Hart's book is an in-depth look at the realities of traveling in the new millennium and managing to stay safe in spite of the many obstacles that may arise.

Focusing on important principles for individuals and families to help prepare themselves for real-life encounters, the author lays out a detailed yet easy-to-understand plan for the readers to follow and make a part of their traveling and everyday routines.

Earnest Hart Jr. is a world-class martial arts champion, physical fitness trainer, actor, and seminar specialist. He regularly presents workshops and lectures, captivating his audiences with details of his life experiences and providing them with straight talk about their personal safety. For workshop and lecture information, contact the author: *www.earnesthart.com*.

Index

A

actual confrontation, 160
Advance Person, 94-95
air marshals, 47
airplane safety, 44
Airport Safety, 43-44, 48
airport security, 42, 92
air rage, 44-45
antiques, 79-80
assassination, 89, 105, 117-18
ATM Safety, 130
avoidance, 156
awareness
   degrees of, 162
   sense of, 16, 66, 123-24
   situational, 164
   skills, 62, 97, 162, 164, 181

B

bell captain, 108-9
Best, Ben, 69
blackmail, 115, 117
black widow, 113-17
body language, 17-18, 160, 162, 166, 178
boxing, 157
buddy system, 124
bump and rob, 35
Bureau of Consular Affairs, 76
burglary, 21-24, 26
buses, 39
business executive, 87-88, 96, 120
business travel, 86, 90, 95
   choosing a safe vehicle, 100-101
   dealing with surveillance, 112

how to detect a surveillance team, 97
preparing for, 91
on private plane/jet, 93
reacting to vehicle attack, 102-4
safe socializing, 111-12
safety during flight, 92
using vehicles as weapons, 104-5
vehicle safety, 98-99
Business Travel Safety, 87-88, 95
bus/train terminal safety, 40

C

car accident, 35-36
car bomb, 106-7
carjackers, 34-35, 83, 100
carjacking, 32, 34-35, 83, 89, 153
Car Safety, 32-33
car trouble, 34
car vandalism, 84
Center for Defense Information (CDI), 47
cocaine, 71
Colombia, 70-71, 90, 118
con artists, 129
confidence, 16-18, 123, 129, 141, 148, 168-70
Consular Information Sheets, 76, 79
counterstrikes, 170
criminal awareness, 163-64
criminals, smart, 21
cruises, 61, 64-65
cruise safety
  off the ship, 65
  on the ship, 63-64

cruise ship security, 62

D

"Death by Murder," 69
De-escalation, 167-68, 177
defense stance, 169
Department of State Publication, 76
distraction scam, 128
doorman, 109
drug possession, 79

E

Electronic tracking, 97
Elevator Safety, 55
Embarrassment, 89
Evasion, 170

F

female travelers, 138
  safety tips for, 141-42
  when going on nightlife, 144-46
  when in buildings, 140-41
  when shopping, 138
  when traveling the streets, 139-40
firearm possession, 79
Florida, 68-69
Francis, Joe, 143

G

"Girls Gone Wild," 143
global positioning system (GPS), 101

grappling, 157, 173, 178
guns, 173
gypsy cabdrivers, 50

H

Hart, Earnest Jr.
   adventure in Los Angeles, 121-22
   incident during a cruise in Jamaica, 61-62
   kickboxing experience in Thailand, 9-13
hijacking, 45-48, 92
home security, 20, 24, 26, 29-31
hostage situation, 45
Hotel Fires, 57, 59
hotel manager, 108
hotel/motel safety, 54-55
   for executives, 108, 110
   receiving mail, 110
hotel room safety, 55-56
hotel security director, 109

J

jujitsu, 157, 173, 178

K

karate, 157
kia, 170
kickboxing, 9-10, 157
kidnapping, 81, 87-90, 98, 118-19
knives, 43, 62, 174

L

light rail system, 51

M

Mace, 174
Mail Screening Procedures, 110
Mental Preparation, 16
MetroLink, 51, 53
Miami, 68
mind-set, proper, 16, 19
muay thai kicks, 11
Murphy's Law, 121

N

9/11, *42*, *43*, *44*, *46*, *47*, *48*
911 emergency system, 21

O

OnStar, 36
Overseas Citizens Services, 76
overseas travel
   avoiding becoming a target of opportunity, 80
   car safety, 36, 83-84
   going through airport security and customs, 78
   planning for, 16, 75-78, 88
   safety in public transportation, 84
   seeking assistance during, 82
   traveling in high risk areas, 81

P

panhandlers, 131
parking lot safety, 132
Parries, 170
peace of mind, 16, 24-26
Pelton, Robert Young
  The World's Most Dangerous Places, 24, 89
Pepper spray, 174-75
Photography, 79
pickpocketings, 40, 84
pickpockets, 51-52, 65, 84, 109
pretravel safety tips, 26-29
prevention, 98-99, 102, 108, 156
private jet, 93
Purse Safety, 127
Purse-snatching, 127

R

ramming, 100, 104-5
ranking
  most dangerous places for business travel, 90
  top ten cities (*The Daily Telegraph*, 2003), 72
  top ten most dangerous countries (Forbes.com, 2010), 70
  top ten most dangerous countries (for tourists), 70
  top ten most dangerous US states, 67
relaxation, 159
rental vehicle, 53, 82
road rage, 37-38

S

scams, 128-29, 154
Self-awareness, 164-66
self-defense, 19, 157-59, 164-65, 181
  ten commandments of, 176-78
  training, 22, 48, 156, 159, 169
senior travelers, 152
  safety tips for, 153-54
  when traveling by car, 155
shopping, 122, 129, 131, 138
Shopping Safety, 131
sidestepping, 170
Somalia, 70-71
street hustler, 129
street safety, 123, 125-26
  dealing with con artists and street hustlers, 129
  rules when confronted by an attacker, 134-35
Street Violence, 89
Stun gun, 175
subway terminal and rail car safety, 52
surveillance, 96-97, 99, 104, 112
  how to detect, 98
  leap frog, 96
  parallel, 96

T

taxicabs, 49-50, 81
taxicab safety, 50-51
terrorism, 70, 80, 86, 88, 112
terrorist profile, 87
terrorists, 45, 87-88, 90, 96, 98-99, 102

Thai boxing, 10
threat assessment, 88, 91
trains, 39
traveling, 15

U

unpredictability, 100

V

vacation safety, 72
Vehicle Inspection Procedures, 107
vehicle safety, 36, 98-99, 133
visualization, 159-61
voice, 18, 168

W

weapons of the body, 172
World's Most Dangerous Places, The (Pelton), 24, 89

Y

Yelling, 170
young travelers
  city smarts for, 152
  in-room safety, 150
  safety tips for age 4–5, *149*
  safety tips for age 6 and above, 150

Edwards Brothers, Inc.
Thorofare, NJ USA
January 13, 2012